Interpretation
of the
Scriptures

Arthur W. Pink

Interpretation
of the
Scriptures

Baker Books
A Division of Baker Book House Co
Grand Rapids, Michigan 49516

© 1972 by Arthur W. Pink

Published by Baker Books
a division of Baker Book House Company
P. O. Box 6287, Grand Rapids, MI 49516-6287

Paperback edition: First printing, June 1977. Second Printing, February 1996

Printed in the United States of America

ISBN 0-8010-7025-2

1

MAN is notoriously a creature of extremes, and nowhere is that fact more evident than in the attitude taken by different ones to this subject. Whereas some have affirmed the Bible is written in such simple language that it calls for no explaining, a far greater number have suffered the papists to persuade them that its contents are so far above the grasp of the natural intellect, its subjects so profound and exalted, its language so abstruse and ambiguous that the common man is quite incapable of understanding it by his own efforts, and therefore that it is the part of wisdom for him to submit his judgment to "holy mother church," who brazenly claims to be the only Divinely authorized and qualified interpreter of God's oracles. Thus does the Papacy withhold God's Word from the laity, and impose her own dogmas and superstitions upon them. For the most part the laity are quite content to have it so, for thereby they are relieved of searching the Scriptures for themselves. Nor is it much better with many Protestants, for in most cases they are too indolent to *study* the Bible for themselves, and believe only what they hear from the pulpits.

The principal passage appealed to by Romanists in an attempt to bolster up their pernicious contention that the Bible is a dangerous book — because of its alleged obscurity — to place in the hands of the common people is II Peter 3:15, 16. Therein the Holy Spirit has told us that the apostle Paul, according to the wisdom given him, spoke in his epistles of "some things hard to be understood, which they that are unlearned and unstable wrest, as they do also the other scriptures, to their own destruction." But as Calvin long ago pointed out, "We are not forbidden to read Paul's epistles because they contain some things difficult to be understood, but that, on the contrary, they are commended to us, providing we have a calm and teachable mind." It is also to be noted that this verse says "some things" and not "many," and that they are "hard" and *not* "incapable of being understood"! Moreover, the obscurity is not in them, but in the depravity of our nature which resists the holy requirements of God, and the pride of our hearts which disdains seeking enlightenment from Him. The "unlearned" here refers not to illiteracy, but to being untaught of God; and the "unstable" are those with no settled convictions, who, like weathervanes, turn according to whatever wind of doctrine blows upon them.

On the other hand, there are some misguided souls who have suffered the pendulum to swing to the apposite extreme, denying that the Scriptures need any interpreting. They aver they have been written for simple souls, saying what they mean and meaning what they say. They insist that the Bible requires to be *believed* and not explained. But it is wrong to pit those two things against each other: both are necessary.

7

God does not ask for blind credence from us, but an intelligent faith, and for that three things are indispensable: that His Word should be read (or heard), understood, and personally appropriated. None other than Christ Himself gave exhortation, "Whoso readeth, let him *understand*" (Matt. 24:15) — the mind must be exercised upon what is read. That a certain amount of understanding is imperative appears further from our Lord's parable of the Sower and the Seed: "When any one heareth the word of the kingdom, and understandeth it not, then cometh the wicked one, and catcheth away that which was sown in his heart . . . but he that received seed into the good ground is he that heareth the word, and understandeth it" (Matt. 13:19, 23). Then let us spare no pains to arrive at the meaning of what we read, for what *use* can we make of what is unintelligible to us?

Others take the position that the only Interpreter they need, the only One adequate for the task, is the Holy Spirit. They quote: "But ye have an unction from the Holy One, and ye know all things . . . but the anointing which ye have received of Him abideth in you, and ye need not that any *man* teach you" (I John 2:20, 27). To declare that I need none but the Holy Spirit to teach me may sound very honoring to Him, but is it true? Like all human assertions that one requires to be *tested*, for nothing must be taken for granted where spiritual things are concerned. We answer that it is not, otherwise Christ makes superfluous provision by giving "pastors and teachers *for* the perfecting of the saints, for the work of the ministry" (Eph. 4:11, 12). We must ever bear in mind that it is a very short step from trusting God to tempting Him, from faith to presumption (Matt. 4:6, 7). Neither should we forget what is God's common and usual method in supplying the wants of His creatures — mediately and not immediately, by secondary causes and human agent. That pertains as much to the spiritual realm as to the natural. It has pleased God to furnish His people with gifted instructors, and instead of haughtily ignoring them we ought (while *testing* their teaching — Acts 17:11) to accept thankfully whatever help they can afford us.

Far be it from us to write anything which would discourage the young believer from recognizing and realizing his *dependence upon* God, and his need of constantly turning to Him for wisdom from above, particularly so when engaged in reading or meditating upon His Holy Word. Yet he must bear in mind that the Most High does not tie Himself to answer our prayers in any particular manner or way. In some instances He is pleased to illumine our understandings directly and immediately, but more often than not He does so through the instrumentality of others. Thereby He not only hides pride from us individually, but places honor on His own institution, for He has appointed and qualified men to "feed the flock" (I Peter 5:2), "guides over us" whose faith we are bidden to follow (Heb. 13:7). It is true that, on the one hand, God has so written His Word that the wayfaring man, though a fool, should not err therein (Isaiah 35:8); yet, on the other hand, there are "mysteries" and "deep things" (I Cor. 2:10); and while there is "milk" suited to babes there is also "strong meat," which belongs only to those who are of full age (Heb. 5:13, 14).

Turning from the general to the particular let us evince there is a real need for interpretation. First, in order to explain *seeming contradictions.* Thus, "God did *tempt* Abraham, and said unto him . . . Take now thy son . . . and offer him there for a burnt offering" (Gen. 22:1, 2). Now place by the side of that statement the testimony of James 1:13, "Let no man say when he is tempted, I am tempted of God: for God cannot be tempted with evil, neither tempteth He any man." Those verses appear to conflict openly with each other, yet the believer knows that such is not the case, though he may be at a loss to demonstrate that there is no inconsistency in them. It is therefore *the meaning* of those verses which has to be ascertained. Nor is that very difficult. Manifestly the word "tempt" is not used in the same sense in those sentences. The word "tempt" has both a primary and a secondary meaning. Primarily, it signifies to make trial of, to prove, to test. Secondarily, it signifies to allure, seduce, or solicit to evil. Without a shadow of doubt the term is used in Genesis 22:1, in its primary sense, for even though there had been no Divine intervention at the eleventh hour, Abraham had committed no sin in slaying Isaac, since God had bidden him do so.

By the Lord's tempting Abraham on this occasion we are to understand not that He would entice unto evil as Satan does but rather that He made trial of the patriarch's loyalty, affording him an opportunity to display his fear of Him, his faith in Him, his love to Him. When Satan tempts he places an allurement before us with the object of encompassing our downfall; but when God tempts or tests us, He has our welfare at heart. Every trial is thus a temptation, for it serves to make manifest the prevailing disposition of the heart — whether it be holy or unholy. Christ was "in all points tempted like as we are, sin (indwelling) excepted" (Heb. 4:15). His temptation was real, yet there was no conflict within Him (as in us) between good and evil — His inherent holiness repelled Satan's impious suggestions as water does fire. We are to "count it all joy when we fall into divers temptations" or "manifold trials," since they are means of mortifying our lusts, tests of our obedience, opportunities to prove the sufficiency of God's grace. Obviously we should not be called on to rejoice over inducements to sin!

Again, "The Lord is *far* from the wicked" (Prov. 15:29), yet in Acts 17:27, we are told He is *"not far* from every one of us" — words which were addressed to a heathen audience! These two statements seem to contradict one another, yea, unless they be interpreted they *do* so. It has, then, to be ascertained in *what sense* God is "far from" and in what sense He is "not far from" the wicked — *that* is what is meant by "interpretation." Distinction has to be drawn between God's powerful or providential presence and His favorable presence. In His spiritual essence or omnipresence God is ever nigh unto all of His creatures (for He "fills heaven and earth" — Jer. 23:24) sustaining their beings, holding their souls in life (Ps. 64:9), bestowing upon them the mercies of His providence. But since the wicked are far from God in their affections (Ps. 73:27), saying in their hearts "Depart from us: for we desire not the knowledge of Thy ways" (Job 21:14), so His gracious presence is far

from them: He does not manifest Himself to them, has no communion
with them, hears not their prayers ("the proud He knoweth afar off" —
Ps. 138:6), succors them not in the time of their need, and will yet bid
them "depart from Me, ye cursed" (Matt. 25:41). Unto the righteous
God is graciously near: Psalms 34:18; 145:18.

Once more. "If I bear witness of Myself, My witness is not true" (John
5:31) — "though I bear record of Myself, yet My record is true" (John 8:
14). Another pair of opposites! Yet there is no conflict between them
when rightly *interpreted.* In John 5:17-31, Christ was declaring His
sevenfold equality with the Father: first in service, then in will. Verse 19
means He could originate nothing that was contrary to the Father, for
they were of perfect accord (see v. 30). In like manner, He could not
bear witness of Himself *independently* of the Father, for that would be
an act of insubordination. Instead, His own witness was in perfect accord therewith: the Father Himself (v. 37), and the Scriptures (v. 39),
bore testimony to His absolute deity. But in John 8:13, 14, Christ was
making direct reply to the Pharisees, who said His witness was false.
That He emphatically denied, and appealed again to the witness of the
Father (v. 18). Yet again. "I and My Father are one" (John 10:30) —
"My Father is greater than I" (John 14:28). In the former, Christ was
speaking of Himself according to His essential being; in the latter, in
reference to His mediatorial character or official position.

Second, interpretation is necessary to prevent our being misled by the
mere *sound of words.* How many have formed wrong conceptions from
the language used in different verses through their failure to understand
its *sense.* To many it appears impious to place a different meaning upon
a term than what appears to be its obvious signification; yet a sufficient
warning against this should be found in the case of those who have so
fanatically and stubbornly adhered to Christ's words, "this [unleavened
bread] *is* My body," refusing to allow that it must mean "this *represents*
My body" — as "the seven candlesticks which thou sawest *are* [i.e. sym-
bolize] the seven churches" (Rev. 1:20). The error of Universalism,
based upon indefinite terms being given an unlimited meaning, points
further warning. Arminianism errs in the same direction. "That He by
the grace of God should taste death for *every man*" (Heb. 2:9) no more
included Cain, Pharaoh and Judas than "every man" is to be understood
absolutely in Luke 16:16; Romans 12:3; I Corinthians 4:5; and "all men"
in I Timothy 2:4, 6, is no more to be taken as meaning all without exception than it is in Luke 3:15; John 3:26; Acts 22:15.

"Noah was a just man and perfect in his generations" (Gen. 6:9). Of
Job, too, it is said that he was "perfect and upright" (1:1). How many
have allowed themselves to be misled by the sound of those words.
What false concepts have been formed of their import! Those who believe in what they term "the second blessing" or "entire sanctification"
consider they confirm their contention that sinless perfection is attainable
in this life. Yet such a mistake is quite inexcusable, for what is recorded very soon afterwards of those men shows plainly they were very
far from being without moral defect: the one becoming intoxicated, the

other cursing the day of his birth. The word "perfect" in those and similar passages signifies "honest, sincere," being opposed to hypocrisy. "We speak wisdom among them that are perfect" (I Cor. 2:6). There, and in Philippians 3:15, the word signifies "mature" — compare "of full age" in Hebrews 5:14 — as distinct from infantile.

"I will make drunk her princes, and her wise men . . . and they shall sleep *a perpetual sleep,* and not wake, saith the King, whose name is the Lord of hosts" (Jer. 51:57). Those words are cited by gross materialists, who believe in the annihilation of the souls of the wicked. They need not detain us long, for the language is plainly figurative. God was about to execute judgment upon the pride of Babylon, and as a historical fact that mighty city was captured while its king and his courtiers were in a drunken stupor, being slain therein, so that they awoke no more on earth. That "perpetual sleep" *cannot* be understood literally and absolutely is evident from other passages which expressly announce the resurrection of the wicked — Daniel 12:2; John 6:29.

"He hath not beheld iniquity in Jacob, neither hath He seen perverseness in Israel" (Num. 23:21). How often those words have been regarded absolutely, without any regard to their context. They were a part of Balaam's explanation to Balak, why he could not curse Israel so that they should be exterminated by the Midianites. Such language did not mean that Israel was in a sinless state, but that up to that time they were free from any open rebellion against or apostasy from Jehovah. They had not been guilty of any heinous offense like idolatry. They had conducted themselves as to be unfit for cursing and cutting off. But later the Lord *did* see "perverseness" in Israel, and commissioned Babylon to execute His judgment upon them (Isaiah 10). It is unwarrantable to apply this relative statement to the Church absolutely, for God *does* "behold iniquity" in His children, as His chastening rod demonstrates; though He imputes it not unto penal condemnation.

Third, interpretation is needed for the *inserting of an explanatory word* in some passages. Thus in "Thou art of purer eyes than to [approvingly] behold evil, and canst not [condoningly] look on iniquity" (Hab. 1:13). Some such qualifying terms as these are required, otherwise we should make them contradict such a verse as "The eyes of the Lord are in every place, beholding the evil and the good" (Prov. 15:3). God never beholds evil with complacency, but He *does* to requite it. Once more. "For who hath resisted His [secret or decretive] will?" (Rom. 9: 19); "neither did according to His [revealed or preceptive] will" (Luke 12:47) — unless those distinctions be made Scripture would contradict itself. Again, "Blessed are they that [evangelically, i.e., with genuine desire and effort] keep His testimonies" (Ps. 119:2) — for none do so according to the strict rigor of His Law.

For our concluding example of the need for interpretation let us take a very familiar and simple verse: "Jesus Christ *the same* yesterday, and today, and forever" (Heb. 13:8). Does that "say what it means"? Certainly, says the reader; and the writer heartily agrees. But are you sure that you understand *the meaning* of what it says? Has Christ undergone no change since the days of His flesh? Is He the same absolutely today as He was yesterday? Does He still experience bodily hunger, thirst, and weariness? Is He still in "the form of a servant," in a state of humiliation, "the Man of sorrows"? Interpretation is here obviously needed, for there must be a sense in which He *is* still "the same." He is unchanged in His essential Person, in the exercise of His mediatorial office, in His relation unto and attitude toward His Church — loving them with an everlasting love. But He has altered in His humanity, for that has been glorified; and in the position which He now occupies (Matt. 28:18; Acts 2:36). Thus the best known and most elementary verses call for careful examination and prayerful meditation in order to arrive at the meaning of their terms.

2

In the previous chapter we sought to show the *need for* interpretation, that it devolves upon us to ascertain the import of what is meant by every sentence of Holy Writ. What God has *said* to us is of inestimable importance and value, yet what profit can we derive therefrom unless its *significance* is clear to us? The Holy Spirit has given us more than a hint of this by *explaining* the meaning of certain words. Thus, in the very first chapter of the New Testament it is said of Christ, "they shall call His name Emmanuel, which *being interpreted* is, God with us" (Matt. 1:23). And again, "We have found the Messias, which is, being interpreted, the Christ" — margin "the Anointed" (John 1:43). Again, "And they bring Him unto the place Golgotha, which is, being interpreted, The place of a skull" (Mark 15:22). Yet again "Melchisedec, king of Salem . . . first being by interpretation King of righteousness, and after that also King of Salem, which is, King of peace" (Heb. 7:1, 2). Those expressions make it clear that it is essential that we should understand the sense of each word used in the Scriptures. God's Word is made up of words, yet they convey nothing to us while they remain unintelligible. Hence, to ascertain the precise import of what we read should be our first concern.

Before setting forth some of the rules to be observed and the principles to be employed in the interpretation of Scripture, we would point out various things which require to be found in the would-be interpreter himself. Good tools are indeed indispensable for good workmanship, but the best of them are to little purpose in the hands of one who is unqualified to use them. Methods of Bible study are only of relative importance; but the *spirit* in which it is studied is all-important. It calls for no argument to prove that a spiritual book calls for a spiritually minded reader, for "the natural man receiveth not the things of the Spirit of God . . . neither can he know them, because they are spiritually discerned" (I Cor. 2:14). God's Word is a revelation of things which affect our highest interests and everlasting welfare, and it demands both implicit and cordial acceptance. Something more than intellectual training is required: the heart must be right as well as the head. Only where there is honesty of soul and spirituality of heart will there be clearness of vision to perceive the Truth; only then will the mind be capable of discerning the full import of what is read, and understand not only the bare meaning of its words, but the sentiments they are designed to convey, and a suitable response be made by us.

We will repeat here what we wrote in *Studies in the Scriptures* twenty years ago. "There is grave reason to believe that much Bible reading and Bible study of the last few years has been of no spiritual profit to those engaged in it. Yea, we go farther: we greatly fear that in many instances it has proved a curse rather than a blessing. This is strong language, we are well aware, but no stronger than the case calls for. Divine gifts may be misused and Divine mercies abused. That this has been so in the present instance is evidenced by the fruits produced. Even the natural man can (and often does) take up the study of the Scriptures with the same enthusiasm and pleasure as he might one of the sciences. Where this is the case, his store of knowledge is increased, and so also is his pride. Like a chemist engaged in making interesting experiments, the intellectual searcher of the Word is quite elated when he makes some new discovery, yet the joy of the latter is no more spiritual than would be that of the former. So, too, just as the success of the chemist generally increases his sense of self-importance and causes him to look down upon those more ignorant than himself, such alas, has been the case with those who have investigated the subjects of Bible numerics, typology, prophecy. . . ."

Since the imagination of man, like all the other faculties of his moral being, is permeated and vitiated by sin, the ideas it suggests, even when pondering the Divine oracles, are prone to be mistaken and corrupt. It is part of our sinful infirmity that we are unable of ourselves to interpret God's Word aright; but it is part of the gracious office of the Holy Spirit to guide believers into the truth, thereby enabling them to apprehend the Scriptures. This is a distinct and special operation of the Spirit on the minds of God's people, whereby He communicates spiritual wisdom and light unto them, and which is necessary unto their discerning aright the mind of God in His Word, and also their laying hold of the heavenly things found therein. "A distinct operation" we say, by which we mean something *ab extra* or over and above His initial work of quickening; for while it be a blessed fact that at regeneration He has "given us an understanding, that we may know Him that is true" (I John 5:20), yet more is needed in order for us to "know the things that are freely given to us of God" (I Cor. 2:12). This is evident from the case of the apostles, for though they had companied and communed with Christ for the space of three years, yet we are informed that, at a later date, "Then opened He their understanding, that they *might understand* the scriptures" (Luke 24:45).

How what has been just alluded to should impress the Christian himself with the need for holy caution when reading the Word, lest he wrest its contents unto his own injury! How it should humble him before its Author and make him realize his utter dependence upon Him! If the new birth *were* sufficient of itself to capacitate the believer to grasp Divine things, the apostle had never made request for the Colossian saints that they "*might be* filled with the knowledge of God's will in all wisdom and spiritual understanding" (1:9), nor would he have said to his son in the faith, "the Lord give thee understanding in all things" (II Tim. 2:7). There never was a more foolish notion or pernicious idea entertained than that the holy mysteries of the Gospel so lie within the province of human reason that they may be known profitably and practically without the effectual aid of the blessed Spirit of Truth. Not that He instructs us in any other way than by and through our reason and understanding, for then we should be reduced to irrational creatures; but that He must enlighten our minds, elevate and direct our thoughts, quicken our affections, move our wills, and thereby enable our understandings, if we are to apprehend spiritual things.

Nor does the Holy Spirit's teaching of the individual Christian by any means set aside or render him independent of making diligent and conscientious use of the ministry of the pulpit, for that is an important means appointed by God for the edifying of His people. There is a happy medium between the attitude of the Ethiopian eunuch who, when asked, "Understandest thou what thou readest?" replied, "How can I, except some man should guide me?" (Acts 8:30, 31), and the wrong use made of "ye need not that any man teach you" (I John 2:27) — between a slavish reliance upon human instruments and a haughty independence of those whom Christ has called and qualified to feed His sheep. "Yet is not their understanding of the Truth, their apprehension of it, and faith in it, to rest upon or to be resolved into *their* authority, who are not appointed of God to be 'lords of their faith,' but 'helpers of their joy' (II Cor. 1:24). And therein depends all our interest in that great promise that we shall be 'all taught of God,' for we are not so, unless we do learn from Him those things which He has revealed in His Word" (John Owen).

"And all Thy children shall be taught of the Lord" (Isa. 54:13, and cf. John 6:45). This is one of the great distinguishing marks of the regenerate. There are multitudes of unregenerate religionists who are well versed in the letter of Scripture, thoroughly acquainted with the history and the doctrines of Christianity, but their knowledge came only from *human* media — parents, Sunday school teachers, or their personal reading. Tens of thousands of graceless professors possess an intellectual knowledge of spiritual things which is considerable, sound, and clear; yet they are not Divinely taught, as is evident from the absence of the fruits which ever accompany the same. In like manner, there are a great number of preachers who abhor the errors of Modernism and contend earnestly for the Faith. They were taught in Bible institutes or trained in theological seminaries, yet it is greatly to be feared that they are total strangers to a supernatural work of grace in their souls, and that their knowledge of the Truth is but a notional one, unaccompanied by any heavenly unction, saving power, or transforming effects. By diligent application, and personal effort one may secure a vast amount of scriptural information, and become an able expositor of the Word; but he cannot obtain thereby a heart-affecting and heart-purifying knowledge thereof. None but the Spirit of Truth can write God's Law on my heart, stamp His image on my soul, sanctify me by the Truth.

Here, then, is the first and most essential qualification for understanding and interpreting the Scriptures, namely *a mind illumined by the Holy Spirit*. The need for this is fundamental and universal. Of the Jews we are told, "But even unto this day, when Moses is read, the veil is upon their heart" (II Cor. 3:15). Though the Old Testament be deeply venerated and diligently studied by the "orthodox" section, yet is its spiritual purport unperceived by them. Such also is the case with the Gentiles. There is a veil of *ill-will* over the heart of fallen man for "the carnal mind is enmity against God" (Rom. 8:7). There is a veil of *ignorance* over the mind. As a child may spell out the letters and learn to pronounce words the sense of which he apprehends not, so we may ascertain the literal or grammatical meaning of this Word and yet have no spiritual knowledge of it, and thus belong to that generation of whom it is said "hearing ye shall hear, and shall not understand; and seeing ye shall see, and shall not perceive" (Matt. 13:14). There is a veil of *prejudice* over the affections. "Our hearts are overcast with strong affections of the world, and so cannot clearly judge practical truth" (Manton). That which conflicts with natural interests and calls for the denying of self is unwelcome. There is a veil of *pride* which effectually prevents us seeing ourselves in the mirror of the Word.

Now that veil is not completely removed from the heart at regeneration, hence our vision is yet very imperfect and our capacity to take in the Truth unto spiritual profit very inconsiderable. In his first epistle to the Corinthian church the apostle said, "If any man think that he knoweth any thing, he knoweth nothing yet as he ought to know" (8:2). It is a great mercy when the Christian is made to realize that fact. So long as he remains in this evil world and the corrupt principle of the flesh continues in him, the believer needs to be led and taught by the Spirit. This is very evident from the case of David, for while he declared, "I have more understanding than all my teachers," yet we find him praying to God, "Open Thou mine eyes, that I may behold wondrous things out of Thy law. . . . Teach me, O Lord, the way of Thy statutes. . . . Give me understanding" (Ps. 119:18, 33, 34). Observe that the Psalmist did not complain at the obscurity of God's Law, but realized the fault was in himself. Nor did he make request for new revelations (by dreams or visions), but instead a clearer sight of what was already revealed. Those who are the best and longest taught are always readiest to sit at the feet of Christ and learn of Him (Luke 10:39).

It is to be duly noted that the verb in Psalm 119:18, literally signifies "uncover, unveil mine eyes," which confirms our opening sentence in the last paragraph. God's Word is a spiritual light objectively, but to discern it aright there needs to be sight or light subjectively, for it is only by and in His light that "we see light" (Ps. 36:9). The Bible is here termed "God's Law" because it is clothed with Divine authority, uttering the mandates of His will. It contains not so much good advice, which we are free to accept at our pleasure, but imperious edicts which we reject at our peril. In that Word are "wondrous things" which by the use of mere reason we cannot attain unto. They are the riches of Divine wisdom, which are far above the compass of man's intellect. Those "wondrous things" the believer longs to behold or clearly discern, yet is he quite unable to do so without Divine assistance. Therefore, he prays that God will so unveil his eyes that he may behold them to good purpose, or apprehend them unto faith and obedience — i.e., understand them practically and experientially in the way of duty.

"Behold, God exalteth [elevates the soul above the merely natural] by His power: who teacheth like Him?" (Job 36:22). None; when He instructs, He does so effectually. "I am the Lord thy God which teacheth thee to profit, which leadeth thee by the way that thou shouldest go" (Isa. 48:17): *that* is what His "teaching" consists of — a producing of pious conduct. It is not merely an addition being made to our mental store, but a bestirring of the soul to holy activity. The light which *He* imparts warms the heart, fires the affections. So far from puffing up its recipient, as natural knowledge does, it humbles. It reveals to us our ignorance and stupidity, shows us our sinfulness and worthlessness, and makes the believer little in his own eyes. The Spirits' teaching also gives us clearly to see the utter vanity of the things highly esteemed by the unregenerate, showing us the transitoriness and comparative worthlessness of earthly honors, riches and fame, causing us to hold all temporal things with a light hand. The knowledge which God imparts is a *transforming* one, making us to lay aside hindering weights, to deny ungodliness and worldly lusts, and to live soberly, righteously, and godly in this present world. Beholding the glory of the Lord we are "changed into the same image from glory to glory, even as by the Spirit of the Lord" (II Cor. 3:18).

The very character of Divine teaching demonstrates how urgent is our need of the same. It consists very largely in overcoming our native antipathy for and hostility to Divine things. By nature we have a love of sin and hatred of holiness (John 3:19), and that must be effectually subdued by the power of the Spirit ere we desire the pure milk of the Word — observe what has to be laid aside before we can receive with meekness the ingrafted Word (James 1:21; I Peter 2:1); though it be *our* duty, only *He* can enable us to perform it. By nature we are proud and independent, self-sufficient and confident in our own powers. That evil spirit clings to the Christian to the end of his pilgrimage, and only the Spirit of God can work in him that humility and meekness which are requisite if he is to take the place of a little child before the Word. The love of honor and praise among men is another corrupt affection of our souls, an insuperable obstacle to the admission of the Truth (John 5:44; 12:43), which has to be purged out of us. The fierce and persistent opposition made by Satan to prevent our apprehension of the Word (Matt. 13:19; II Cor. 4:4) is far too powerful for us to resist in our own strength; none but the Lord can deliver us from his evil suggestions and expose his lying sophistries.

Second, *an impartial spirit* is required if we are to discern and apprehend the real teaching of Holy Writ. Nothing more beclouds the judgment than prejudice — none so blind as those who will not see. Particularly is that the case with all who come to the Bible with the object of finding passages which prove "our doctrines." An honest heart is the first quality the Lord predicated of the good-ground hearer (Luke 8:15), and where *that* exists we are not only willing but desirous to have our own views corrected. There can be no advance made in our spiritual apprehension of the Truth until we are ready to submit our ideas and sentiments to the teaching of God's Word. While we cling to our pre-conceived opinions and sectarian partialities, instead of being ready to abandon all beliefs not clearly taught in Scripture, neither praying nor studying can profit the soul. There is nothing which God hates more than insincerity, and we are guilty thereof if, while asking Him to instruct us, we at the same time refuse to relinquish what is erroneous. A thirst for the Truth itself, with a candid determination for it to mold all our thinking and direct our practice, is indispensable if we are to be spiritually enlightened.

Third, *a humble mind*. "This is an eternal and unalterable law of God's appointment, that whoever will learn His mind and will, as revealed in Scripture, must be humble and lowly, renouncing all trust and confidence in themselves. The knowledge of a proud man is the throne of Satan in his mind. To suppose that persons under the predominancy of pride, self-conceit and self-confidence can understand the mind of God in a due manner is to renounce the Scripture, or innumerable positive testimonies to the contrary" (Owen). The Lord Jesus declared that heavenly mysteries are hid from the wise and prudent, but revealed unto babes (Matt. 11:25). Those who assume an attitude of competency, and are wise in their own esteem, remain spiritually ignorant and unenlightened. Whatever knowledge men may acquire by their natural abilities and industry is nothing unto the glory of God, nor to the eternal gain of their souls, for the Spirit refuses to instruct the haughty. "God resisteth the proud" (James 4:6) — "He draws up against him, He prepares Himself, as it were, with His whole force to oppose his progress. A most formidable expression! If God only leaves us unto ourselves, we are all ignorance and darkness; so what must be the dreadful case of those against whom He appears in arms?" (John Newton). But, blessed be His name, He "giveth grace unto the humble" — those of a childlike disposition.

Fourth, *a praying heart*. Since the Bible is different from all other books, it makes demands upon its readers which none other does. What one man has written, another man can master; but only the Inspirer of the Word is competent to interpret it unto us. It is at this very point that so many fail. They approach the Bible as they would any other book, relying on a closeness of attention and diligence of perusal to understand its contents. We must first get down on our knees and cry unto God for light: "Incline my heart unto Thy testimonies . . . give me understanding, that I may learn Thy commandments . . . order my steps in Thy word" (Ps. 119:36, 73, 133). No real progress can be made in our apprehension of the Truth until we realize our deep and constant need of a Divinely anointed eye. "If any of you lack wisdom, let him ask of God, that giveth to all liberally" (James 1:5). It is because they make use of that promise that many a Christian ploughman and simple housewife is taught of the Spirit, while prayerless scholars know not the secret of the Lord. Not only do we need to pray "that which I see not, teach Thou me," but request God to write His Word on our hearts.

Fifth, *a holy design.* Many are deceived in this matter, mistaking an eagerness to acquire scriptural knowledge for a love of the Truth itself. Inquisitiveness to discover what the Bible says is why some read it. A sense of shame to be unable to discover its teaching prompts others. The desire to be familiar with its contents so as to hold their own in an argument moves still others. If it be nothing better than a mere desire to be well versed in its details which causes us to read the Bible, it is more than likely that the garden of our souls will remain barren. The inspiring motive should be *honestly examined.* Do I search the Scriptures in order to become better acquainted with their Author and His will for me? Is the dominating purpose which actuates me that I may grow in grace and in the knowledge of the Lord? Is it that I may ascertain more clearly and fully how I should order the details of my life, so that it will be more pleasing and honoring to Him? Is it that I may be brought into a closer walking with God and the enjoyment of more unbroken communion with Him? Nothing less is a worthy aim than that I may be conformed to and transformed by its holy teaching.

In this chapter we have dealt only with the elementary side of our subject, nevertheless of what is of basic importance, and which few attend unto. Even in the palmy days of the Puritans, Owen had to complain, "the number is very small of those who diligently, humbly, and conscientiously endeavour to learn the Truth from the voice of God in the Scriptures, or to grow wise in the mysteries of the Gospel by such ways as wherein alone that wisdom is attainable. And is it any wonder if many, the greater number of men, wander after vain imaginations of their own or others?" May it not be so with those who read this chapter.

3

CHAPTER 2 dealt with some of the more elementary yet essential qualifications which must needs be found in any who would enter into the spiritual meaning of Holy Writ. It was therefore suited to all the people of God in general. But in this we propose to treat of those things which have a more particular bearing upon those whom God has called to preach and teach His Word: those whose whole time and energies are to be devoted to seeking the spiritual and eternal welfare of souls, and the better equipping of themselves for that most blessed, solemn, and important work. Their principal tasks are to proclaim God's Truth and to exemplify and commend their message by diligently endeavoring to practise what they preach, setting before their hearers a personal example of practical godliness. Since it be the Truth they are to preach, no pains must be spared in seeing to it that no error be intermingled therewith, that it is the pure milk of the Word they are giving forth. To preach error instead of Truth is not only grievously to dishonor God and His Word, but will mislead and poison the minds of the hearers or readers.

The preacher's task is both the most honorable and the most solemn of any calling, the most privileged and at the same time the most responsible one. He professes to be a servant of the Lord Jesus Christ, a messenger sent forth by the Most High. To misrepresent his Master, to preach any other Gospel than His, to falsify the message which God has committed to his trust, is the sin of sins, which brings down upon him the anathema of heaven (Gal. 1:8), and will be visited with the sorest punishment awaiting any creature. Scripture is plain that the heaviest measure of Divine wrath is reserved for unfaithful preachers (Matt. 23: 14; Jude 13). Therefore the warning is given, "be not many masters, knowing that we shall receive the greater condemnation" (James 3:1) if unfaithful to our trust. Every minister of the Gospel will yet have to render a full account of his stewardship unto the One whom he claims called him to feed His sheep (Heb. 13:17), to answer for the souls who were committed to his charge. If he fails to diligently warn the wicked, and he dies in his iniquity, God declares "his blood will I require at thine hand" (Ezek. 3:18).

Thus the chief and constant duty of the preacher is to conform unto that injunction, "Study to show thyself approved unto God, a workman that needeth not to be ashamed, rightly dividing the word of truth" (II Tim. 2:15). In the whole of Scripture there is no exhortation addressed to preachers which is of greater importance than that one, and few equal. Doubtless that is why Satan has been so active in seeking to obscure its first two clauses by raising such a cloud of dust over the last one. The Greek word for "study" here signifies "give diligence": spare no efforts, but make it your paramount concern and constant endeavor to please your Master. Seek not the smiles and flatteries of worms of the earth, but the approbation of the Lord. *That* is to take precedence of everything else: unless it is, attention to the second thing mentioned will be in vain. Entirely subordinate all other aims to commending *thyself* unto God — thine own heart and character, thy dealings with and walk before Him, ordering all thy ways according to His revealed will. What are your "service," your ministrations, worth, if He be displeased *with thee?*

"A workman that needeth not to be ashamed." Be conscientious, diligent, faithful, in the use you make of your time and the talents God has entrusted to you. Give unremitting heed to that precept. "Whatsoever thy hand findeth to do, do it with thy might" (Eccles. 9:10) — put your very best into it. Be industrious and assiduous, not careless and slovenly. See how well you can do each thing, and not how quickly. The Greek word for "workman" is also translated "laborer," and in twentieth-century English might well be rendered "toiler." The ministry is no place for triflers and idlers, but for those who are prepared to spend and be spent in the cause of Christ. The preacher ought to work harder than the miner, and to spend more hours per week in his study than does the man of business in his office. A workman is the very opposite of a shirker. If the preacher is to show himself approved unto God and be a workman that needeth not to be ashamed, then he will have to labor while others sleep, and do so until he sweats mentally.

"Meditate upon these things; give thyself wholly to them; that thy profiting may appear to all. Take heed *unto thyself,* and unto the doctrine; *continue* in them: for in doing this thou shalt both save thyself, and them that hear thee" (I Tim. 4:15, 16). This is another part of the. mandate which Christ has laid upon His official servants, and a most comprehensive and exacting one it is. He requires them to put their hearts into the work, to give the whole of their thoughts to it, to lay themselves completely out in it, to devote all their time and strength thereto. They are to keep clear of all secular affairs and worldly employments, and show all diligence in the task assigned them. That it is an arduous task appears from the different designations given them. They are called "soldiers" to denote the exertions and fatigue which attend the proper discharge of their calling; "overseers and watchmen" to intimate the care and concern which accompany their office; "shepherds and teachers" to signify the various duties of leading and feeding those committed to their charge. But first and formost they are to take heed to their *personal* growth in grace and piety, if they would minister effectually unto others.

Particularly does the minister need to attend unto this injunction "take heed unto thyself" in his study of the Scriptures, reading them devotionally ere he does so professionally; that is, seeking their application and blessing to his own soul before searching for sermonic materials. As the saintly Hervey expressed it, "Thus may we always be affected when we study the oracles of Truth. Study them, not as cold critics, who are only to judge of their meaning, but as persons deeply interested in all they contain. Who are particularly addressed in every exhortation, and directed in every precept. Whose are the promises, and to whom belong the precious privileges. When we are enabled thus to *realize and appropriate* the contents of that invaluable Book, then shall we taste the sweetness and feel the power of the Scriptures. Then shall we know by happy experience that our Divine Master's words are not barely sounds and syllables, but that they are spirit and they are life." No man can be constantly giving out — that which is fresh and savory — unless he be continually taking in. That which he is to declare unto others is what his own ears have first heard, his own eyes have seen, his own hands have handled (I John 1:1, 2).

The mere *quoting* of Scripture in the pulpit is not sufficient — people can become familiar with the letter of the Word by reading it at home; it is the *expounding and application of it* which are so much needed, "And Paul, as his manner was . . . reasoned with them out of the scriptures, opening and alleging, that Christ must needs have suffered, and risen again from the dead" (Acts 17:2, 3). But to "open" the Scriptures helpfully to the saints requires something more than a few months' training in a Bible institute, or a year or two in a seminary. None but those who have been personally taught of God in the hard school of experience are qualified so to "open" the Word that Divine light is cast upon the spiritual problems of the believer, for while Scripture interprets experience, experience is often the best interpreter of Scripture. "The *heart* of the wise teacheth his mouth, and addeth learning to his lips" (Prov. 16:23), and that "learning" cannot be acquired in any of man's schools. No one can learn what humility is by means of the concordance, nor secure more faith by studying certain passages of Scripture. The one is acquired through painful discoveries of the plague of our hearts, and the other is increased by a deepening acquaintance with God. We must ourselves be comforted of Him before we can comfort others (II Cor. 1: 4).

"To seek after mere *notions* of Truth, without an endeavor after an experience of its power in our hearts, is not the way to increase our understanding in spiritual things. He alone is in a posture to learn from God, who sincerely gives up his mind, conscience, and affections to the power and rule of what is revealed unto him. Men may have in their study of the Scriptures other ends also, as the profit and edification *of others*. But if this conforming of their own souls unto the power of the Word be not fixed in the first place in their minds they do not strive lawfully, nor will they be crowned. And if at any time, when we study the Word, we have not this design expressly in our minds, yet if upon the discovery of any truth we endeavour not to have the likeness of it in our own hearts, we lose our principal advantage by it" (John Owen). It is much to be feared that many preachers will have reason to lament in the day to come, "They made me the keeper of the vineyards; but mine own vineyard have I not kept" (Song of Sol. 1:6) — like a chef preparing meals for others and himself starved.

While the preacher is to ponder the Word devotionally, he is also to read it *studiously*. If he is to become able to feed his flock with "the finest of the wheat" (Psalm 81:16), then he must needs study it diligently and daily, and that to the end of his life. Alas, that so many preachers abandon their habit of study as soon as they are ordained! The Bible is an inexhaustible mind of spiritual treasure, and the more its riches are opened to us (by hard digging) the more we realize how much there is yet unpossessed, and how little we really understand what has been received. "If any man think that he knoweth any thing, he knoweth nothing yet as he ought to know" (I Cor. 8:2).

The Word of God cannot be understood without a constant and laborious study, without a careful and prayerful scrutiny of its contents. This is not to say that it is recondite and obscure. No, it is as plain and intelligible as in the nature of things it can be, adopted in the best possible manner to give instruction in the holy and profound things of which it treats. But none can be instructed by the best possible means of instruction who will not take pains with the same. Promise of understanding is made not to the dilatory and indolent, but to the diligent and earnest, to those who seek for spiritual treasure (Prov. 2:3, 5). The Scriptures have to be searched, searched daily, persistently and perseveringly, if the minister is to become thoroughly familiar with *the whole* of what God has revealed, and if he is to set before his hearers "a feast of fat things." Of the wise preacher it is said, "he still taught the people knowledge, yea, he gave good heed, and sought out," even "sought to find out acceptable words" (Eccles. 12:9, 10), as if his whole soul was engaged in the discovery of the best mode as well as the best substance of instruction.

No preacher should be content with being anything less than "a man mighty in the scriptures" (Acts 18:24). But to attain thereunto he must subordinate all other interests. An old writer quaintly said, "The preacher should be with his time as the miser is with his gold — saving it with care, and spending it with caution." He must also remind himself constantly *whose* Book it is he is about to take up, so that he ever handles it with the utmost reverence, and can aver "my heart standeth in awe of Thy word" (Ps. 119:161). He must approach it in lowly-mindedness, for it is only unto such that the Lord "giveth more grace." He must ever come to it in the spirit of prayer, crying "that which I see not teach Thou me" (Job 34:32): the enlightening grace of the Spirit will often open mysteries to the meek and dependent which remain closed to the most learned and scholarly. A holy heart is equally indispensable for the reception of supernatural truth, for the understanding is clarified by the purifying of the heart. Let there also be a humble expectation of Divine help, for "according unto your faith be it unto you" holds good here too.

It is only by giving heed to the things which have been pointed out in the preceding paragraphs that the necessary foundations are laid for any man's becoming a competent expositor. The task before him is to unfold, with clearness and accuracy, the Word of God. His business is entirely exegetical — to bring out the true meaning of each passage he deals with, whether it accords with his own preconceptions or no. As it is the work of the translator to convey the real sense of the Hebrew and Greek into English, so the interpreter's is to apprehend and communicate the precise ideas which the language of the Bible was meant to impart. As the renowned Bengel so well expressed it, "An expositor should be like the maker of a well: who puts no water into it, but makes it his object to let the water flow, *without* diversion, stoppage, or defilement." In other words, he must not take the slightest liberty with the sacred text, nor give it a meaning which it will not legitimately bear; neither modifying its force nor superimposing upon it anything of his own, but seeking to give out its true import.

To comply with what has just been said calls for an unbiased approach, an honest heart, and a spirit of fidelity, on the part of the interpreter. "Nothing should be elicited from the text but what is yielded by the fair and grammatical explanation of its language" (P. Fairbairn). It is easy to assent to that dictum, but often difficult to put it into practice. A personal shrinking from what condemns the preacher, a sectarian bias of mind, the desire to please his hearers, have caused not a few to evade the plain force of certain passages, and to foist on them significations which are quite foreign to their meaning. Said Luther, "We must not make God's Word mean what *we* wish. We must not bend *it*, but allow it to *bend us*, and give it the honor of being better than we can make it." Anything other than that is highly reprehensible. Great care needs ever to be taken that we do not expound our own minds instead of God's. Nothing can be more blameworthy than for a man to profess to be uttering a "Thus saith the Lord" when he is merely expressing his own thoughts. Yet who is there who has not, unwittingly, done so?

If the druggist is required by law to follow exactly the doctor's prescription, if military officers must transmit the orders of their commanders verbatim or suffer severe penalties, how much more incumbent is it for one dealing with Divine and eternal things to adhere strictly to his text book! The interpreter's task is to emulate those described in Nehemiah 8:8, of whom it is said "they read in the book in the law of the Lord God distinctly, and *gave the sense,* and caused them to understand the reading." The reference is to those who had returned to Palestine from Babylon. While in captivity they had gradually ceased to use Hebrew as their spoken language. Aramaic displacing it. Hence there was a real need to explain the Hebrew words in which the Law was written (cf. Neh. 13:23, 24). Yet the recording of this incident intimates that it is of permanent importance, and has a message for us. In the good providence of God there is little need today for the preacher to explain the Hebrew and the Greek, since we already possess a reliable translation of them into our own mother tongue — though occasionally, yet very sparingly, he may do so. But his principal business is to "give the sense" of the English Bible and cause his hearers to "understand" its contents. His responsibility is to adhere strictly to that injunction, "let him speak My word faithfully. What is the chaff of the wheat? saith the Lord" (Jer. 23:28).

4

THE preacher should be, above everything else, a man of the Book, thoroughly versed in the contents of God's Word, one who is able to bring forth out of his treasure "things new and old" (Matt. 13:52). The Bible is to be his sole text-book, and from its living waters he is to drink deeply and daily. Personally, we use nothing else than the English Authorized Version and Young's concordance, with an occasional reference to the Greek Interlinear and the American Revised Version. Commentaries we consult only *after* we have made a first-hand and exhaustive study of a passage. We strongly urge young preachers to be much on their guard against allowing commentaries to become a substitute for, instead of a supplement to, their own minute and full examination and pondering of Holy Writ. As there is a happy mean between imagining either that the Bible is so plain and simple that anyone can understand it or so difficult and profound that it would be a waste of time for the average person to read it, so there is between being mainly dependent on the labors of others and simply echoes of their ideas and utterly disparaging that light and help which may be obtained from God's servants of the past.

It is at the feet of God that the preacher must take his place, learning from Him the meaning of His Word, waiting upon Him to open its mysteries, looking to Him for his message. Nowhere but in the Scriptures can he ascertain what is pleasing or displeasing unto the Lord. There alone are opened the secrets of Divine wisdom, of which the philosopher and scientist know nothing. And as the great Dutch Puritan rightly pointed out, "Whatever is not drawn from them, whatever is not built upon them, whatever does not most exactly accord with them, however it may recommend itself by the appearance of the most sublime wisdom, or rest on ancient tradition and consent of learned men, or the weight of plausible arguments, it is vain, futile, and, in short, a lie. 'To the law and to the testimony: if they speak not according to this word it is because there is no light in them.' Let the theologian delight in those sacred Oracles: let him exercise himself in them day and night, meditate in them, draw all his wisdom from them. Let him compass all his thoughts on them, let him embrace nothing in religion which he does not find there" (Herman Witsius).

1. Coming now to those principles which are to guide the student in his efforts to interpret God's Word, we place first and foremost the need for recognizing the *inter-relation and mutual dependence of* the Old and New Testaments. We do so because error at this point inevitably results in a serious misunderstanding and perverting of not a little in the later Scriptures. We do not propose to enter into a refutation of the modern heresy of "dispensationalism," but to treat of this section of our subject

constructively. After a long and careful comparison of the writings of that school with *The Institutes* of Calvin, and our observation of the kind of fruit borne by the one and the other, it is our conviction that that eminent reformer was far more deeply taught by the Holy Spirit than those who claimed to receive so much "new light on God's Word" a century ago. We would therefore urge every preacher who possesses Calvin's *Institutes* to give his very best attention to its two chapters on "The Similarity of the Old and New Testaments" and "The Difference of the Two Testaments."

The *similarity* of the two Testaments is much greater and more vital than their dissimilarity. The same triune God is revealed in each, the same way of salvation is set forth, the same standard of holiness is exhibited, the same eternal destinies of the righteous and the wicked made known. The New has all its roots in the Old, so that much in the one is unintelligible apart from the other. Not only is a knowledge of the history of the patriarchs and of the institutions of Judaism indispensable for an understanding of many details in the Gospels and the Epistles, but its terms and ideas are identical. That it is entirely unwarrantable for us to suppose that the message proclaimed by the Lord Jesus was something new or radically different from the early communications of God appears from His emphatic warning: "Think not that I am come to destroy the law, or the prophets: I am not come to destroy, but to fulfil" (Matt. 5:17) — to vindicate and substantiate them, to free them from human perversions and misrepresentations, and to make good what they demanded and announced. So far from there being any antagonism between the teaching of Christ and Divine messengers who preceded Him, when He enunciated "the golden law" He stated, "for this is the law and the prophets" (Matt. 7:12).

Most certainly there was no conflict between the testimony of the apostles and that of their Master, for He had expressly enjoined them to teach their converts "to observe all things whatsoever I *have* [not shall!] commanded you" (Matt. 28:20). Nor did the doctrinal system of Paul differ in any wise from that enunciated in the Old Testament. At the very beginning of the first epistle bearing his name he is particular to inform us that the Gospel unto which God had separated him was none other than the one "He had promised afore by His prophets in the holy scriptures" (Rom. 1:1, 2); and when he stated that the righteousness of God was now revealed apart from the Law, he was careful to add, "being witnessed by the law and the prophets" (3:21). When he vindicated his teaching on justification by faith without the deeds of the Law, he did so by appealing to the case of Abraham and the testimony of David (Rom. 4). When he admonished the Corinthians against being lulled into a false sense of security because of the spiritual gifts which had been bestowed upon them, he reminded them of the Israelites who had been highly favored of God, yet that did not keep them from His displeasure when they sinned, even though they "did all eat *the same* spiritual meat; and did drink the same spiritual drink" (I Cor. 10:1-5). And when illustrating important practical truth, he cites the history of Abraham's two sons (Gal. 4:22-31).

In many respects the New Testament is a continuation of and a complement to the Old. The difference between the old and new covenants referred to in Hebrews is a relative and not an absolute one. The contrast is not really between two opposites, but rather between a gradation from the lower to the higher plane — the one preparing for the other. While some have erred in too much Judaizing Christianity, others have entertained far too carnal a conception of Judaism, failing to perceive the *spiritual* elements in it, and that under it God was then as truly administering the blessings of the everlasting covenant unto those whom He had chosen in Christ as He is now, yea, that He had done so from Abel onwards. Rightly, then, did Calvin rebuke the madness of our modern dispensationalists when reproving those of their forerunners who appeared in his day, saying, "Now what would be more absurd than that Abraham should be the father of all the faithful, and not possess even the lowest place among them? But he cannot be excluded from the number, even from the most honorable station, without the destruction of the Church."

Whether the speaker is Christ or one of His apostles, at almost every vital point he clinches his argument by an appeal to the Old Testament scriptures, proof-texts therefrom being found in almost every page in the New. Innumerable examples might be adduced to show that both the ideas and the language of the former have given their impress to the latter — more than six hundred expressions in the one occurring in the other. Every clause in the "Magnificat" (Luke 1:46-55) and even in the family prayer (Matt. 6:9-13) is drawn from the Old Testament. It therefore behoves the student to give equal attention to *both* of the principal divisions of the Bible, not only thoroughly familiarizing himself with the latter but endeavoring to drink deeply of the spirit of the first, in order to fit him for understanding the second. Unless he does so, it will be impossible for him to apprehend aright much in the Gospels and Epistles. Not only is a knowledge of the types necessary to comprehend the antitypes — for what would "Christ our passover is sacrificed for us" (I Cor. 5:7) mean to one ignorant of Exodus 12; and how much in Hebrews 9 and 10 is intelligible apart from Leviticus 16? — but many important words of the New Testament can be correctly defined only by referring back to their usage in the Old Testament: such as "firstborn, redeem, propitiation," etc.

That there must be a fundamental harmony between Judaism and Christianity appears in the fact that the same God is the Author of both, and is unchanging in His perfections and the principles of His government. The former was indeed addressed more to the outward man, was transacted under visible forms and relations, and had respect primarily to a worldly sanctuary and earthly inheritance; nevertheless, they were all of them a "shadow of heavenly things" (Heb. 8:5; 10:1). "In the New Testament we have a higher, yet very closely related, exhibition of truth and duty than in the Old, which involves both the agreements and differences of the two covenants. The agreements lie deeper and concern the more essential elements of the two economies; the differences are of a more circumstantial and formal nature" (Fairbairn). Personally, we would say that the principal variations appear in that in the one we have promise and prediction, in the other performance and fulfilment: first the types and shadows (the "blade"), then the reality and substance or "full corn in the ear." The Christian dispensation excels the Mosaic in a fuller and clearer manifestation of God's perfections (I John 2:8), in a more abundant effusion of the Spirit (John 7:39; Acts 2:3), in its wider extent (Matt. 28:19, 20), and in a larger measure of liberty (Rom. 8:15; Gal. 4:2-7).

2. The second principle which the expositor must make a most careful study of is that of *scriptural quotation*. Not a little help in ascertaining the right laws of interpretation may be obtained from diligently observing *the manner in which and the purpose for which the* Old Testament is cited in the New. There can be little room for doubt that the record which the Holy Spirit has supplied of the way in which our Lord and His apostles understood and applied the Old Testament was as much designed to throw light *generally* on how the Old Testament is to be used by us as it was to furnish instruction on the particular points for the sake of which passages in the Law or the prophets were more immediately appealed to. By examining closely the words quoted and the sense given to them in the New Testament, we shall not only be delivered from a slavish literalism, but be better enabled to perceive the *fullness* of God's words and the varied application which may be legitimately made of them. A wide, but generally neglected, field is open for exploration, but instead of endeavoring here to make a thorough canvass of the same, we shall simply supply a few illustrations.

In Matthew 8:16, we are told that on a certain occasion Christ "healed all that were sick," and then under the guidance of the Holy Spirit the evangelist added, "that it might be fulfilled which was spoken by Esaias the prophet [namely in 53:4], saying, Himself took our infirmities and bare our sicknesses." Such a use of that Messianic prediction is most illuminating, intimating as it does that it had a *wider* signification than the making of atonement for the sins of His people, namely that during the days of His public ministry Christ entered sympathetically into the condition of the sufferers, and took upon His spirit the sorrows and pains of those to whom He ministered, that His miracles of healing cost Him much in the way of compassion and endurance. He was personally afflicted by their afflictions. Christ began His mediatorial work of removing the evil which sin had brought into the world by curing those bodily ailments which were the fruits of sin, and by so doing shadowed forth the greater work He was to accomplish at the cross. The *connection* between the one and the other was more plainly indicated when He said alternatively to the sick of the palsy, "Thy sins be forgiven thee" and "arise, take up thy bed and go unto thine house" (Matt. 9: 2, 6).

Consider next how Christ used the Old Testament to refute the materialists of His day. The Sadducees held the notion that the soul and body are so closely allied that if one perishes the other must (Acts 23: 8). They saw the body die, and therefrom concluded that the soul had also. Very striking indeed is it to behold incarnate wisdom reasoning with them on their own ground. This He did by quoting from Exodus 3, where Jehovah had said unto Moses, "I am the God of Abraham, and the God of Isaac, and the God of Jacob." But *wherein* were those words to the point? What was there in them which exposed the error of the Sadducees? Nothing explicitly, but much implicitly. From them Christ drew the conclusion that "God is not the God of the dead, but of the living" (Matt. 22:32). It was not that He had been their "God," but that He was so still — "I *am* their God," therefore they still lived. Since their spirits and souls were yet alive, their bodies must be raised in due course, for being their "God" guaranteed that He would be to them and do for them all that such a relation called for, and not leave a part of their nature to be a prey of corruption. Therein Christ established the important principle of interpretation that we may draw any clear and necessary *inference* from a passage, provided it clashes not with any definite statement of Holy Writ.

In Romans 4:11-18, we have a remarkable example of apostolic *reasoning* from two short passages in Genesis, wherein God made promise unto Abraham that he should be a father of many nations (17:5) and that in his seed should all the nations of the earth be blessed (22:18). Since these assurances were given to the patriarch simply as a believer, *before* the Divine appointment of circumcision, Paul drew the logical conclusion that they pertained to Jews and Gentiles alike, providing they believed as he did and thereby had imputed to them the righteousness of Christ, that the good of those promises belonged unto *all* who "walk in the steps of his faith." Therein we are plainly taught that the "seed" of blessing mentioned in those ancient prophecies was essentially of a *spiritual* kind (cf. Gal 3:7-9; 14:29), including all the members of the household of faith, wherever they be found. As Stifler pertinently remarked, "Abraham is called *father* neither in a physical sense nor a spiritual: he is father in that he is head of the faith clan, and so the normal type." In Romans 9:6-13, the apostle was equally express in *excluding* from the good of those promises the merely natural descendants of Abraham.

Romans 10:5-9, supplies a striking illustration of this principle in the way that the apostle "opened" Deuteronomy 30:11-14. His design was to draw off the Jews from regarding obedience to the Law as necessary unto justification (Rom. 10:2, 3). He did so by producing an argument from the writings of Moses, wherein a distinction was drawn between the righteousness of the Law and the righteousness of faith. The Jews had rejected Christ because He came not to them in the way of their carnal expectations, and therfore refused the grace tendered by Him. They considered the Messiah was far off, when in fact He was "nigh" them. There was no need, then, for them to ascend to heaven, for Christ had come down from thence; nor to descend into the deep, for He had risen from the dead. The apostle was not merely accommodating to his purpose the language of Deuteronomy 30, but showing its evangelical drift. As Manton said, "The whole of that chapter is a sermon of evangelical repentance" (see vv. 1, 2). It obviously looked forward to a time after Christ's ascension when Israel would be dispersed among the nations, so that the words of Moses there were strictly applicable to this Gospel dispensation. The substance of verses 11-14 is that the knowledge of God's will is freely accessible, so that none are required to do the impossible.

In Romans 10:18, more than a hint is given of the profound depths of God's Word and the wide breadth of its application. "But I say, Have they not heard [the Gospel, though they obeyed it not – v. 16]? Yes verily, their sound went into all the earth, and their words unto the ends of the world" – quoted from Psalm 19:4. The publication of the Gospel was not restricted (Col. 1:5, 6), but was as general and free as the Divine declarations of the heavens (Psalm 19:1). "The universal revelation of God in nature was a providential prediction of the universal proclamation of the Gospel. If the former was not gratuitous, but founded in the nature of God, so must the latter be. The manifestation of God in nature is for all His creatures to whom it is made, in pledge of their participation in the clearer and higher revelations" (Hengstenberg). Not only did Old Testament prophecy announce that the Gospel should be given to the whole world, but the heavens *mystically* declared the same thing. The heavens speak not to one nation only, but the whole human race! If men did not believe it was not because they had not heard. Another example of the *mystical* signification of certain scriptures is found in I Corinthians 9:9, 10.

In Galatians 4:24, the inspired pen of Paul informs us that certain domestic incidents in the household of Abraham "are in allegory," that Hagar and Sarah represented "the two covenants," and that their sons prefigured the kind of worshippers those covenants were fitted to produce. But for that Divine revelation unto and through the apostle we should never have known that in those facts of history God had concealed a prophetic mystery, that those domestic occurrences prophetically shadowed forth vitally important transactions of the future, that they illustrated great doctrinal truths and exemplified the difference in conduct of spiritual slaves and spiritual freemen. Yet such was the case, as the apostle showed by opening to us the occult meaning of those events. They were a parable in action: God so shaped the affairs of Abraham's family as to typify things of vast magnitude. The two sons were ordained to foreshadow those who should be born from above and those born after the flesh – that even Abraham's natural descendants were but Ishmaelites in spirit, strangers to the promise. While Paul's example here is certainly *no precedent* for the expositor to give free rein to his imagination and make Old Testament episodes teach anything he pleases, it *does* intimate that God so ordered the lives of the patriarchs as to afford lessons of great spiritual value.

We have, above, designedly selected a variety of examples, and from them the diligent student (but not so the hurried reader) will discover some valuable Divine hints and helps on *how* the Scriptures are to be understood, and the principles *by which* they are to be interpreted. Let them be reread and carefully pondered.

3. Constant care must be diligently taken strictly to conform all our interpretations to *the Analogy of Faith*, or, as Romans 12:6, expresses it, "let us prophesy according to the proportion of faith." Charles Hodge, who, for doctrinal soundness, spiritual scholarship, and critical acumen, is unsurpassed, states that the original and proper meaning of the word "prophet" is *interpreter* — one who declares the will of God, who explains His mind to others. He also says that the word rendered "proportion" may mean either proportion, or measure, rule, standard. Since "faith" in this verse must be taken *objectively* (for there were "prophets" like Balaam and Caiphas, who were devoid of any inward or saving faith), then this important expression signifies that the interpreter of God's mind must be most particular and scrupulous in seeing to it that he ever does so in accordance with the revealed standard He has given us. Thus "faith" here is used in the same sense as in such passages as "the faith" in Galatians 1:23; I Timothy 4:1, etc.; namely the "one faith" of Ephesians 4:5, "the faith which was once delivered unto the saints" (Jude 3) — the written Word of God.

The exposition made of any verse in Holy Writ must be in entire agreement with the Analogy of Faith, or that system of truth which God has made known unto His people. That, of course, calls for a comprehensive knowledge of the contents of the Bible — sure proof that no "novice" is qualified to preach to or attempt to teach others. Such comprehensive knowledge can be obtained only by a systematic and constant reading of the Word itself — and only then is any man fitted to weigh the writings of others! Since all Scripture is given by inspiration of God, there are no contradictions therein; thus it obviously follows that any explanation given of a passage which clashes with the plain teaching of other verses is manifestly erroneous. In order for any interpretation to be valid, it must be in perfect keeping with the scheme of Divine Truth. One part of the Truth is mutually related to and dependent upon others, and therefore there is full accord between them. As Bengel said of the books of Scripture, "They indicate together one beautiful, harmonious and gloriously connected system of Truth."

5

To say that all our interpretations must conform strictly to the Analogy of Faith may sound very simple and obvious, yet it is surprising to find how many not only unskilled but experienced men depart therefrom. Of course, those who covet "originality," and have a penchant for bringing out something new or startling (especially from obscure passages) without regard to this basic principle, are sure to err. But as J. Owen observed, "Whilst we sincerely attend unto this rule, we are in no danger of sinfully corrupting the Word of God, although we shall not arrive unto its proper meaning in every place." For example, when we learn that "God is a spirit" (John 4:24), incorporeal and invisible, that prevents us from misunderstanding those passages where eyes and ears, hands and feet are ascribed to Him; and when we are informed that with Him there is "no variableness, neither shadow of turning" (James 1:17), we know that when He is said to "repent" He speaks after the manner of men. Likewise, when Psalm 19:11, and other verses make promise of the saints being rewarded for their gracious tempers and good works, other passages show that such recompense is not because of merit, but is bestowed by Divine grace.

No verse is to be explained in a manner which conflicts with what is taught, plainly and uniformly, in the Scriptures as a whole, and which whole is set before us as the alone rule of our faith and obedience. This requires from the expositor not only a knowledge of the general sense of the Bible, but also that he takes the trouble to collect and compare all the passages which treat of or have a definite bearing upon the immediate point before him, so that he may obtain the *full* mind of the Spirit thereon. Having done that, any passage which is still obscure or doubtful to him must be interpreted by those which are clear. No doctrine is to be founded on a single passage, like the Mormons base on I Corinthians 15:29, their error of members of that cult being baptized for their ancestors; or as the papists appeal to James 5:14, 15, for their dogma of "extreme unction." It is only in the mouths of two or three witnesses that any truth is established, as our Lord insisted in His ministry: John 5:31-39; 8:16-18. Care is to be taken that no important teaching is based alone on any type, figurative expression, or even parable; instead, *they* are to be used only in *illustrating* plain and literal passages.

Let it, then, be settled in the mind of the expositor that no scripture is to be interpreted without regard to the relation in which it stands to other parts. Adherence to this fundamental rule will preserve from the wresting of many a verse. Thus, when we hear Christ saying, "My Father is greater than I" (John 14:28), attention to His previous declaration, "I and My Father are one" (John 10:31), will preclude any idea that He was, in His essential person, in any wise inferior; therefore the reference in John 14:28, *must* refer to His mediatorial office, wherein He was subservient to the Father's will. "Must," we say, for the Son is none other than "the mighty God" (Isa. 9:6), "the true God" (I John 5:20). Again, such words as "be baptized, and wash away thy sins" (Acts 22: 16) must not be understood in a way that conflicts with "the blood of Jesus Christ His Son cleanseth us from all sin" (I John 1:7), but regarded as a *symbolical* "washing" only. "To reconcile all things unto Himself" (Col. 1:20) cannot teach universalism, or every passage affirming the eternal punishment of the lost would be contradicted. I John 3:9, must be understood in a way consistent with I John 1:8.

4. The need for paying close attention to *the context* is also a matter of first importance. Not only must each statement of Scripture be explained in full harmony with the general Analogy of Faith, but more specifically, in complete agreement with the plain sense and tenor of the passage of which it forms a part. That "plain sense" must be diligently searched for. Few things have contributed more to erroneous interpretations than the ignoring of this obvious principle. By divorcing a verse from its setting or singling out a single clause, one may "prove" not only absurdities but real falsities by the very words of Scripture. For instance, "hear the church" is not an exhortation bidding the laity submit their judgments unto clerics, but, as Matthew 18:17, shows, the local assembly must decide the issue when a trespassing brother refuses to be amenable to private counsel. As another has pointed out, "An ingenious and disingenuous mind can select certain detached verses of Scripture, and then combine them in the most arbitrary manner, so that while they indeed are all the very words of Scripture, yet at the same time, they express the thoughts of the compiler and not the Holy Spirit's."

Much help is obtained in ascertaining the precise significance of certain expressions by observing the circumstances and *occasion* of their utterance. Through failure to do so, many a sermonizer has failed to perceive the real force of those well-known words "Open Thou my lips; and my mouth shall show forth Thy praise" (Ps. 51:15). David's mouth had been closed by sin and non-confession, and thereby the Spirit quenched! Now that he had put matters right with the Lord, he longed for Him to unstop his shame-covered lips. The spiritual significance of an event is often perceived by noting, *its connection*. A striking illustration of this is found in Matthew 8:23-26, which, be it borne in mind, has an application unto us. The key to it is found in the last clause of verse 23 and in reading verses 19-22. The order of thought there is very suggestive: the whole passage treats of "following" Christ, and verses 23-26 supply a typical picture of the character of the disciple's path through a stormy world: encountering trials, difficulties and dangers; and it often *appears* that the Lord is "asleep" — unmindful of or indifferent to our peril! In reality it is a testing of faith, a showing us that He requires to be waited on, that He is our only recourse, sufficient for every storm!

The parable recorded in Luke 15:3-32, cannot possibly be interpreted aright if its context be ignored. What needless perplexity has been occasioned and diversity among the commentators concerning the *identity* of the ninety-nine sheep left in the wilderness (defined as "just persons who need no repentance") and the "elder son" (who complained at the generous treatment accorded his brother), through failure to use the key we observe that this one parable (in three parts) was not spoken by Christ to the disciples, but addressed to His enemies. It was given in reply to the Pharisees and scribes who had murmured because our Lord received sinners and ate with them. His design was to expose the condition of their hearts, and to vindicate His own gracious actions. He did so by portraying the lost condition of His carping critics, and by making known the ground on which He received sinners into fellowship with Himself, and revealing the Divine operations which issue in that blessed result. Once those broad facts be apprehended, there is no difficulty in understanding the details of the parable.

Two distinct and sharply contrasted classes are set before us in Luke 15:1, 2: the despised publicans and sinners who, from a deep sense of need, were attracted to Christ; and the proud and self-satisfied Pharisees and scribes. In each of the three parts of the parable the same two classes are in view, and in that order. First, the good Shepherd seeks and secures His lost sheep, for it is *His work* which is the basis of salvation; the ninety and nine, who in their own estimation needed no repentance, figured the self-righteous Pharisee — left in "the wilderness," in contrast with the sheep brought "home." In the second, the secret operations of the Spirit in the heart (under the figure of a woman *inside* the house) are described, and by means of the "light" the lost coin is recovered — the other nine being left to themselves. In the third, the one sought out by the Shepherd, illumined by the Spirit, is seen with the Father; whereas the older son (who boasted "neither transgressed I at any time Thy commandment") figures the Pharisee — *a stranger to* the feasting and rejoicing! Learn from this the importance of observing to whom a passage is addressed, the circumstances and occasion when uttered, the central design of the speaker or writer, *before* attempting to interpret its details.

Every verse beginning with the word "For" requires us to trace the connection: usually it has the force of "because," supplying proof of a preceding statement. Likewise the expression "For this cause" and words like "wherefore and therefore" call for close attention, so that we may have before us the promise from which the conclusion is drawn. The widespread misunderstanding of II Corinthians 5:17, supplies an example of what happens when there is carelessness at this point. Nine times out of ten its opening "Therefore" is not quoted, and through failure to understand *its* meaning an entirely wrong sense is given to "if any man be in Christ, he is a new creature: old things are passed away; behold, all things are become new." That prefatory "therefore" indicates that this verse is not to be considered as a thing apart, complete in itself, but rather as closely connected with something foregoing. On turning back to the previous verse we find it too begins with the word "wherefore," which at once shows that this passage is a didactic or doctrinal one, and neither a biographical one which delineates the experience of the soul nor a hortatory one calling unto the performance of some duty.

It should be carefully noted that the "any man" of II Corinthians 5:17, shows it is not describing some exceptional attainment of a favored few, nor depicting mature Christians only, but rather is postulating something which is common to *all* the regenerate. As a matter of fact, the verse is not treating of Christian experience at all, but of the new relationship into which regeneration brings us. It would take us too far afield now to supply detailed answers to the questions: On what particular subject was the apostle writing? What required him to take it up? What was his special design on this occasion? Suffice it to say, he was refuting his Judaizing traducers and cutting the ground from under their feet. In verses 14-16, he insists that union with Christ results in judicial death to natural relations, wherein all fleshly distinctions of Jew and Gentile cease; yea, brings us on to new or resurrection ground, producing a new standing before God. As members of a new creation, we are under an entirely *new covenant*, and for us the limitations and restrictions of the old covenant are "passed away." It is the principal design of the epistle to the Hebrews to make *this* fact fully manifest.

5. Equally necessary is it for the interpreter to determine *the scope* of each passage, i.e., its coherence with what precedes and follows. Sometimes this can best be done by duly noting *the particular book* in which it is found. Notably is this the case with some in *Hebrews*. How many a Christian, who has had a bad fall or been stayed in a course of backsliding, has, after his repentance, needlessly tortured himself by such verses as 6:4-6; 10:26-31! We say needlessly, for those verses were addressed to a very different class, one whose case was quite otherwise. Those Hebrews occupied a *unique* position. Reared under Judaism, they had espoused the Gospel; but later were distressed and shaken because of the non-realization of the carnal hopes they entertained of the Messiah, and the sore persecution they were then suffering, and were sorely tempted to abandon their Christian profession and return to Judaism. In the passages mentioned above they were plainly warned that such a course would be fatal. Thus to apply those passages to backslidden Christians is entirely unwarrantable, making a use of them which is quite foreign to their scope and design.

Sometimes the key to a passage is to be discovered by observing *in which part* of a book it occurs. A pertinent example of this is found in Romans 2:6-10, which has been grievously wrested by not a few. The grand theme of that epistle is "the righteousness of God" — stated in 1: 16, 17. Its first division runs from 1:18, to 3:21, wherein the universal need for God's righteousness is demonstrated. Its second runs from 3:21, to 5:1, in which the manifestation of God's righteousness is set forth. Its third, the imputation of God's righteousness: 5:1, to 8:39. In 1:18-32, the apostle establishes the guilt of the Gentile world, and in chapter 2 that of the Jew. In its first sixteen verses he states the principles which will operate at the Great Assize, and in verses 17-24 makes direct application of them to the favored nation. Those principles are as

ASSIZE = JUDGEMENT

follows: (1) God's judgment will proceed on the ground that man stands self-condemned (v. 1); (2) it will be according to the real state of the case (v. 2); (3) mercy abused increases guilt (vv. 3-5); (4) deeds, not external relations or lip profession, will decide the issue (vv. 6-10); (5) God will be impartial, showing no favoritism (v. 11); (6) full account will be taken of the various degrees of light enjoyed by different men (vv. 11-15); (7) the judgment will be executed by Jesus Christ (v. 16).

From that brief analysis (which exhibits the *scope* of the passage) it is quite evident that the apostle was *not* making known the way of salvation when he declared, "Who will render to every man according to his deeds: To them who by patient continuance in well doing seek for glory and honor and immortality, eternal life" (vv. 6, 7). So far from affirming that fallen men could secure everlasting felicity by their own well-doing or obedience to God, his design was the very opposite. His purpose was to show what the holy Law of God required, and that that requirement would be insisted upon in the Day of Judgment. Since his depraved nature makes it impossible for any man, Jew or Gentile, to render perfect and continual obedience to the Divine Law, then the utter hopelessness of his case is made apparent, and his dire need to look outside himself unto the righteousness of God in Christ is plainly evinced.

Another passage where inattention to *its scope* has resulted in false doctrine being drawn from it is I Corinthians 3:11-15. Appeal is frequently made to it in support of the dangerous delusion that there is a class of real Christians who have forfeited all "reward" for the future, having *no* good works to their credit; yet will enter heaven. Such a concept is grossly insulting to the Holy Spirit, for it implies that He performs a miracle of grace in the soul, indwells that person, yet that he brings forth no spiritual fruit. Such a grotesque idea is utterly contrary to the Analogy of Faith, for Ephesians 2:10, tells us that those whom God saves by grace through faith are "His workmanship, created in Christ Jesus unto good works." Those who walk not in good works are *unsaved*, for "faith without works is dead" (James 2:20). Scripture declares, "Verily *there is* a reward for the righteous" (Psalm 58:11), that "every [regenerated] man shall have praise of God" (I Cor. 4:5), which certainly could not be the case if some of them are but cumberers of the ground.

Not only is this erroneous interpretation highly dishonoring to God and at direct variance with the plain teaching of other scriptures, but it is refuted by the *context*. In order to understand I Corinthians 3:11-15, verses 1-10 must be heeded — so as to determine *the subject* which the apostle is treating. At the beginning of chapter 3 Paul returns to the charge he had made against the Corinthians in 1:11, where he reproved them for pitting one servant of God against another, with the resultant divisions — the principal occasion of his writing to them. In 3:3, he points out that such conduct evinced their carnality. He reminds them that both himself and Apollos were "*but* ministers" (v. 5). He had merely planted and Apollos watered — it was God who gave the increase. Since neither of them was "any thing" unless God deigned to bless his labors (v. 7), what madness it was to make an idol of a mere instrument! Thus it is clear, beyond any doubt, that the opening verses of I Corinthians 3 treat of *the official ministry* of God's servants. It is plainer still in the Greek, for the word "man" occurs nowhere in the passage, "every man" being literally "every *one*," i.e., of the particular class referred to.

The same subject is continued in verse 8, though there be diversity in the work of God's servants (one evangelistic, another indoctrinating), yet their commission is from the same Master and their mutual aim the good of souls; therefore it is sinful folly to array one against or exalt him above another. Though Christ has distributed different gifts to His servants and allotted them a variety of ministry, "each shall receive his own reward." The building itself is *God's,* ministers being the workmen (v. 9). In verse 10 Paul refers to the *ministerial* "foundation" he had laid (see Eph. 2:20), and what follows concerns the *materials* used by builders who came after him. If those materials (their preaching) honored Christ and edified saints, they would endure and be rewarded. But if instead the preacher used for his themes the increase in crime, the menace of the bomb, the latest doings of the Jews, etc., such worthless rubbish would be burned up in the Day to come and be unrewarded. Thus it is *the materials used by preachers* in their public ministrations, and *not* the walk of private Christians, which is here in view.

6

THE word "interpretation" has in this connection both a stricter or narrower meaning and a looser or wider one. In the former sense, it signifies to bring out the grammatical force of the passage; in the latter, to explain its spiritual purport. If the expositor confine himself rigidly to the technical rules of exegesis, though he may be of some service to the pedant, he will afford little practical help to the rank and file of God's people. To discourse upon the chemical properties of food will not feed a starving man, neither will tracing out the roots of the Hebrew and Greek words (necessary though that be in its proper place) the better enable Christ's followers to fight the good fight of faith. That remark connotes neither that we despise scholarship on the one hand nor that we hold any brief for those who would give free rein to their imagination when handling the Word of God. Rather do we mean that the chief aim of the expositor should be to bring together the Truth and the hearts of his hearers or readers, that the former may have a vitalizing, edifying, transforming effect upon the latter.

In the preceding articles of this series it has been pointed out that the interpreter's task is to emulate those described in Nehemiah 8:8, of whom it is said, "they read in the book in the law of God distinctly, and *gave the sense,* and caused them to understand the reading," and to do *that* the preacher must needs spend many hours every week in his study. Each word in his text must be given its precise and definite meaning according to its general scriptural usage (unless there be very clear intimation to the contrary in the passage before him), or otherwise it would be arbitrary licence, and he would expound God's oracles not by their own terms but by his own fancies or preconceived ideas. The laws of language must never be violated or the meanings of words changed to suit ourselves. We are not to evacuate the true force and import of any term, but to explain it on sound principles, and not by forced constructions or Jesuitical evasions.

The task of the interpreter is to determine, by strict exegetical investigation, the exact import of the words used by the Holy Spirit, and, as far as he possibly can, give forth God's thoughts in his own language. It is to ascertain and fix the exact meaning of the terms used in Holy Writ and scrupulously to avoid the interjection of his personal opinions. He must insert nothing of his own, but simply endeavor to give the real sense of each passage before him. On the one hand, he must not ignore, conceal, or withhold anything that is manifestly in it; on the other hand, he must not add to or twist anything therein to suit his own caprice. Scripture must be allowed to speak for itself, and it *does so* only so far as the preacher sets forth its genuine import. Not only is he to explain its *terms,* but also the nature of the *ideas* they express, otherwise he is apt to make use of scriptural terms and yet give them an unscriptural sense. One may discover with accuracy the meaning of each word in a passage, and yet, from some misconception of its scope or bias in his own mind, have a faulty apprehension of what the passage really teaches.

Carelessness which would not be tolerated in any other connection is, alas, freely indulged in with the Bible. Artists who are most particular in selecting their colors when painting a natural object are often most remiss when assaying to portray a sacred one. Thus Noah's ark is represented as having a number of windows in its sides, whereas it had but one, and that on the top! The dove which came to him after the flood had subsided is pictured with an olive *branch* instead of a "leaf" (Gen. 8:11) in its mouth! The infant Moses in the ark of bulrushes is depicted with a winsome smile on his face instead of tears (Exod. 2:6)! Let no such criminal disregard to the *details* of Holy Scripture mark the expositor. Instead, let the utmost care and pains be taken to ensure accuracy, by scrutinizing every detail, weighing each jot and tittle. The word for "*search* the scriptures" (John 5:39) signifies diligently to track out, as the hunter does the spoor of animals. The interpreter's job is to bring out *the sense* and not merely the sound of the Word.

In enumerating, describing, and illustrating some of the laws or rules which are to govern the interpreter, we have already considered: First, the need for recognizing and being regulated by the interrelation and mutual dependence of the Old and New Testaments. Second, the importance and helpfulness of observing how quotations are made from the Old in the New: the manner in which and purposes for which they are cited. Third, the absolute necessity for strictly conforming all our interpretations to the general Analogy of Faith: that each verse is to be explained in full harmony with that system of Truth which God has made known to us: that any exposition is invalid if it clashes with what is taught elsewhere in the Bible. Fourth, the necessity of paying close attention to the whole context of any passage under consideration. Fifth, the value of ascertaining *the scope* of each passage, and the particular *aspect* of Truth presented therein.

There is not a little in the Sermon on the Mount which forcibly illustrates this rule, for many of its statements have been grievously misunderstood through failure to perceive their scope or design. Thus, when our Lord declared, "Ye have heard that it was said by them of old time, Thou shalt not commit adultery; but I say unto you, That whosoever looketh on a woman to lust after her hath committed adultery with her already in his heart" (Matt. 5:27, 28), it has been supposed that He was setting forth a *higher standard* of moral purity than the one enunciated from Sinai. But such a concept is at direct variance with His design. After solemnly affirming (in v. 17) that so far from its being His mission to destroy the Law or the prophets He had come to fulfil them (i.e., enforce and comply with their requirements), He certainly would not immediately after pit Himself against their teaching. No, from verse 21 onwards He was engaged in making known that righteousness which He required in the citizens of His kingdom, which exceeded the righteousness "of the scribes and Pharisees," who were retailing the dogmas of the rabbis, who had "made the commandment of God of none effect" by their traditions (Matt. 15:6).

Christ did not say, "Ye know what *God* said at Sinai," but "ye have heard that it was said by *them* of old time," which makes it unmistakably clear that He was opposing the teaching of the elders who had restricted the seventh commandment of the Decalogue to the bare act of unlawful intercourse with a married woman; insisting that it required conformity from the inward affections, prohibiting all impure thoughts and desires of the heart. There is much in Matthew 5-7 which cannot be rightly apprehended except our Lord's principal object and design in this address be clearly perceived: until then its plainest statements are more or less obscure and its most pertinent illustrations irrelevant. It was not the *actual* teaching of the Law and prophets which Christ was here rebutting, but the erroneous conclusions which religious teachers had drawn therefrom and the false notions based on them, and which were being so dogmatically promulgated at that time. The sharp edge of the Spirit's sword had been blunted by a rabbinical toning down of its precepts, thereby placing a construction upon them which rendered them objectionable to the unregenerate.

"Ye have heard that it hath been said, An eye for an eye, and a tooth for a tooth. But I say unto you, That ye resist not evil: but whosoever shall smite thee on thy right cheek, turn to him the other also" (vv. 38, 39) supplies another example of the need for ascertaining the scope of a passage before attempting to explain it. Through failure to do so many have quite missed the force of this contrast. It has been supposed that our Lord was here enjoining a more merciful code of conduct than that which was exacted under the Mosaic economy; yet if the reader turns to Deuteronomy 19:17-21, he will find that those verses gave instruction to Israel's "judges": that they were not to be governed by sentiment, but to administer strict justice to the evil-doer — "eye for eye," etc. But this statute, which pertains only to the magistrate enforcing *judicial* retribution, had been perverted by the Pharisees, giving it a *general* application, thereby teaching that each man was warranted in taking the law into his own hands. Our Lord here forbade the inflicting of *private revenge*, and in so doing maintained the clear teaching of the Old Testament (see Exod. 23:4, 5; Lev. 19:18; Prov. 24:29; 25:21, 22, which expressly forbade the exercise of personal malice and retaliation).

"Therefore whosoever heareth these sayings of Mine, and doeth them, I will liken him unto a wise man, which built his house upon a rock: And the rain descended and the floods came, and the wind blew, and beat upon that house; and it fell not: for it was founded upon a rock" (Matt. 7:24, 25). How many sermons have had read into them from those verses what is not there, and failed sadly to bring out what *is* in them, through not understanding their scope. Christ was not there engaged in proclaiming the Gospel of the grace of God and revealing the alone ground of a sinner's acceptance with Him, but was making a practical and searching application of the sermon He was here completing.

The opening "Therefore" at once intimates that He was drawing a conclusion from all He had previously said. In the preceding verses Christ was not describing meritmongers or declaiming against those who trusted in good works and religious performances for their salvation, but was exhorting His hearers to enter in at the strait gate (vv. 13, 14), warning against false prophets (vv. 15-20), denouncing an empty profession. In the verse immediately before (v. 23), so far from presenting Himself as the Redeemer, tenderly wooing sinners, He is seen as the Judge, saying to hypocrites, "Depart from Me, ye that work iniquity."

In view of what has just been pointed out, it would be, to say the least, a strange place for Christ to introduce the Evangel and announce that His own finished work was the only saving foundation for sinners to rest their souls upon. Not only would that give no meaning to the introductory "Therefore," but it would not cohere with what immediately follows where, instead of pointing out our need of trusting in His atoning blood, Christ showed how indispensable it is that we *render obedience* to His precepts. True indeed that there is no redemption for any soul except through "faith in His blood" (Rom. 3:25), but that is not what He was here treating of. Rather was He insisting that not everyone who said unto Him, "Lord, Lord," should enter into His kingdom, but "he that doeth the will of My Father which is in heaven" (v. 21). In other words, He was testing profession, demanding reality: that genuine faith produces good works. They who think themselves to be savingly trusting in the blood of the Lamb while disregarding His commandments are fatally deceiving themselves. Christ did not here liken the one who heard and *believed* His sayings to a wise man who built his house secure on a rock, but instead the one who "heareth and *doeth them*" — as in verse 26, the builder on the sand is one who hears His sayings "and doeth them not."

"Therefore we conclude that a man is justified by faith without the deeds of the law" (Rom. 3:28): "Ye see then how that by works a man is justified, and not by faith only" (James 2:24). Unless the *scope* of each writer be clearly apprehended, those two statements flatly contradict each other. Romans 3:28, is a conclusion from what had been advanced in verses 21-27 — all boasting before God being rendered impossible by the Divine method of salvation. From the very nature of the case, if justification before God be by faith, then it must be by faith alone — without the mingling of anything meritorious of ours. James 2:24, as is clear from verses 17, 18 and 26, is not treating of how the sinner obtains acceptance with God, but how such a one supplies *proof* of his acceptance. Paul was rebutting that legalistic tendency which leads men to go about and "establish their own righteousness" by works; James was contending against that spirit of licentious antinomianism which causes others to pervert the Gospel and insist that good works are not essential for any purpose. Paul was refuting meritmongers who repudiated salvation by grace alone; James was maintaining that grace works through righteousness and transforms its subjects: showing the worthlessness of a dead faith which produces naught but a windy profession. The faithful servant of God will ever alternate in warning his hearers against legalism on the one hand and libertarianism on the other.

6. *The need of interpreting Scripture by Scripture.* The general principle is expressed in the well-known words "comparing spiritual things with spiritual" (I Cor. 2:13), for while the preceding clause has reference more especially to the Divine inspiration by which the apostle taught, as the authoritative mouthpiece of the Lord, yet both verses 12 and 14 treat of the *understanding* of spiritual things, and therefore we consider that the last clause of verse 13 has a double force. The Greek word rendered "comparing" is used in the Septuagint translation of the Old Testament again and again, to express the act of interpreting dreams and enigmas, and C. Hodge paraphrases "comparing spiritual things with spiritual" by "*explaining* the things of the Spirit in the words of the Spirit," pointing out that the word "spiritual" has no substantive connected with it, and thus most naturally agrees with "words" in the former sentence. For these reasons we consider that I Corinthians 2:13, enunciates a most valuable and important rule for the understanding and interpreting of God's Word, namely that one part of it is to be explained by another, for the setting side by side of spiritual things serves to illuminate and illustrate one another, and thereby is their perfect harmony demonstrated. Something more than a confused or vague knowledge of the Scriptures is to be sought after: the ascertaining that one part of the Truth is in full accord with other parts makes manifest their unity — as the curtains in the taberncale were linked together by loops.

To a very large extent, and far more so than any uninspired book, the Bible is a self-explaining volume: not only because it records the performance of its promises and the fulfilment of its prophecies, not only because its types and antitypes mutually unfold each other, but because all its fundamental truths may be discovered by means of its own contents, without reference to anything *ab extra* or outside itself. When difficulty be experienced in one passage it may be resolved by a comparison and examination of other passages, where the same or similar words occur, or where the same or similar subjects are dealt with at greater length or explained more clearly. For example, that vitally important expression "the righteousness of God" in Romans 1:17 — every other place where it occurs in Paul's epistles must be carefully weighed before we can be sure of its exact meaning, and having done so there is no need to consult heathen authors. Not only is this to be done with each word of note, but its parts and derivatives, adjuncts and cognates, are to be searched out in every instance, for often light will thereby be cast upon the same. That God intended us to study His Word thus is evident from the *absence* of any system of classification or arrangement of information being supplied us on any subject.

The principal subjects treated in the Scriptures are presented to us more or less piecemeal, being scattered over its pages and made known under various aspects, some clearly and fully, others more remotely and tersely: in different connections and with different accompaniments in the several passages where they occur. This was designed by God in His manifold wisdom to make us search His Word. It is evident that if we are to apprehend His fully made known mind on any particular subject we must collect and collate all passages in which it is adverted to, or in which a similar thought or sentiment is expressed; and by this method we may be assured that if we conduct our investigation in a right spirit, and with diligence and perseverance, we shall arrive at a clear knowledge of His revealed will. The Bible is somewhat like a mosaic, whose fragments are scattered here and there through the Word, and those fragments have to be gathered by us and carefully fitted together if we are to obtain the complete picture of any one of its innumerable objects. There are many places in the Scriptures which can be understood only by the explanations and amplifications furnished by other passages.

7

In His grace and wisdom God has fully provided against our forming misconceptions of any part of His Truth, by employing a great variety of synonymous terms and different modes of expression. Just as our varied senses, though each imperfect, are effective in conveying to our minds a real impression of the outside world by means of their *joint operation,* so the different and supplementary communications of God through the many penmen of Scripture enable us to revise our first impressions and enlarge our views of Divine things, widening the horizon of Truth and permitting us to obtain a more adequate conception of the same. What one writer expresses in figurative language, another sets forth in plain words. While one prophet stresses the goodness and mercy of God, another emphasizes His severity and justice. If one evangelist exhibits the perfections of Christ's humanity, another makes prominent His deity; if one portrays Him as the lowly servant, another reveals Him as the majestic King. Does one apostle dwell upon the efficacy of faith, then another shows the value of love, while a third reminds us that faith and love are but empty words unless they produce spiritual fruit? Thus Scripture requires to be studied as a whole, and one part of it compared with another, if we are to obtain a proper apprehension of Divine revelation. Very much in the New Testament is unintelligible apart from the Old: not a little in the Epistles requires the Gospels and the Acts for its elucidation.

More specifically. The value of comparing Scripture with Scripture appears in the *corroboration* which is afforded. Not that they require any authentication, for they are the Word of Him who cannot lie, and must be received as such, by a bowing unreservedly to their Divine authority. No, but rather that our faith therein may be the more firmly and fully fixed. As the system of double entry in bookkeeping provides a sure check for the auditor, so in the mouths of two or three witnesses the Truth is established. Thus we find our Lord employing this method in John 5, making manifest the excuselessness of the Jews' unbelief in His deity by appealing to the different witnesses who attested the same (vv. 32-39). So His apostle in the synagogue at Antioch, when establishing the fact of His resurrection, was not content to cite only Psalm 2:7, in proof, but appealed also to Psalm 16:10 (Acts 13:33-36). So too in his Epistles: a striking example of which is found in Romans 15, where, after affirming that "Jesus Christ was a minister of the circumcision for the truth of God, to confirm the promises made unto the fathers," he added, "And that the Gentiles might glorify God for His mercy," quoting Psalm 18:49, in proof; but since this was a controverted point among the Jews, he added further evidence — note his "And again" at the beginning of verses 10, 11, 12. So also "by *two* immutable things [God's promise and oath] . . . we might have strong consolation" (Heb. 6:18).

Scripture needs to be compared with Scripture for the purpose of *elucidation*. "If thine enemy be hungry, give him bread to eat; and if he be thirsty, give him water to drink; for thou shalt heap coals of fire upon his head, and the Lord shall reward thee" (Prov. 25:21, 22). The commentators are about equally divided between two entirely diverse views of what is signified by the figurative expression "coals of fire" being heaped upon the head of an enemy by treating him kindly: one class contending that it means the aggravating of his guilt, the other insisting that it imports the destroying of a spirit of enmity in him and the winning of his good will. By carefully comparing the context in which this passage is quoted in Romans 12:20, the controversy is decided, for that makes it clear that the latter is the true interpretation, for the spirit of the Gospel entirely rules out of court the performing of any actions which would ensure the doom of an adversary. Yet an appeal to the New Testament ought not to be necessary in order to expose the error of the other explanation, for the Law equally with the Gospel enjoined love to our neighbor and kindness to an enemy. As John tells us in his First Epistle, when inculcating the law of love he was giving "no new commandment," but one which they had had from the beginning; but now it was enforced by a new example and motive (2:7, 8).

"He could there do no mighty work, save that He laid His hands upon a few sick folk, and healed them" (Mark 6:5). So determined are some Arminians to deny the almightiness of God and the invincibility of His will that they have appealed to this passage in proof that the power of His incarnate Son was limited, and that there were occasions when His merciful designs were thwarted by man. But a comparison of the parallel passage in Matthew 13:54-58, at once gives the lie to such a blasphemous assertion, for we are there told "He did not many mighty works *there* because of *their unbelief*." Thus it was not any limitation in Himself, but something in them, which restrained Him. In other words, He was actuated by a sense of propriety. The emphasis both in Mark 6:5, and Matthew 13:58, is on the word "there," for, as the context shows, this occurred at Nazareth where He was lightly esteemed. To have performed prodigies of power before those who regarded Him with contempt had, in principle, been casting pearls before swine; as it had been unfitting to have wrought miracles to gratify the curiosity of Herod (Luke 23:8) — elsewhere He did many supernatural works. In Genesis 19:22, the Lord could not destroy Sodom until Lot had escaped from it, while in Jeremiah 44:22, He "could no longer bear" the evil doings of Israel — it was moral propriety, not physical inability.

Comparison is useful also for the purpose of *amplification*. Not only does one Scripture support and illuminate another, but very often one passage supplements and augments another. A simple yet striking example of this is seen in what is known as the Parable of the Sower, but which perhaps might be more aptly designated the Parable of the Seed and the Soils. The deep importance of this parable is intimated to us by the Holy Spirit in His having moved Matthew, Mark and Luke to record the same. The three accounts of it contain some striking variations, and they need to be carefully compared together in order to obtain the complete pictures therein set forth. Its scope is revealed in Luke 8:18: "Take heed therefore *how* ye hear." It speaks not from the standpoint of the effectuation of the Divine counsels, but is the enforcing of human responsibility. This is made unmistakably clear from what is said of the one who received the seed into good ground — the fruitful hearer of the Word. Christ did not describe him as one "in whom a work of Divine grace is wrought," or "whose heart had been made receptive by the supernatural operations of the Spirit," but rather as he that received the Word in "an honest and good heart." True indeed the quickening work of the Spirit must precede anyone's so receiving the Word as to become fruitful (Acts 16:14), but that is not the particular aspect of the Truth which our Lord was *here* presenting; instead, He was showing what the hearer himself must seek grace to do if he is to bring forth fruit to God's glory.

The sower himself is almost lost sight of(!), nearly all of the details of the parable being concerned with the various kinds of soil into which the seed fell, rendering it either unproductive or yielding an increase. In it Christ set forth the reception which the preaching of the Word meets with. He likened the world to a field, which He divided into four parts, according to its different kinds of ground. In His interpretation He defined the diverse soils as representing different kinds of people who hear the preaching of the Word, and it solemnly behoves each of us diligently to search himself, that he may ascertain for sure to which of those grounds he belongs. Those four classes — from the descriptions given of the soils and the explanations Christ furnished of them — may be labelled, respectively, the hard-hearted, the shallow-hearted, the half-hearted, and the whole-hearted. In the first, the seed obtained no hold; in the second, it secured no root; in the third, it was allowed no room; in the fourth, it had all three, and therefore yielded an increase. The same four classes have been found in all generations among those who have sat under the preaching of God's Word, and they exist in probably every church and assembly on earth today; nor is it difficult to distinguish them, if we measure professing Christians by what the Lord predicated of each one.

The first is the "wayside" hearer, whose heart is entirely unreceptive — as the highway is beaten down and hardened by the traffic of the world. The seed penetrates not such ground, and "the fowls of the air" catch it away. Christ explained this as being a picture of one who "understandeth not the word" (though it be his duty to take pains and do so — I Cor. 8:2), and the wicked one takes away the Word out of his heart — Luke 8 adds "lest they believe and be saved." The second is the "stony-ground" hearer — i.e., ground with a rock foundation over which lies but a thin layer of soil. Since there be no depth of earth the seed obtained no root, and the scorching sun caused it soon to wither away. This is a representation of the superficial hearer, whose emotions are stirred, but who lacks any searching of conscience and deep convictions. He receives the Word with a natural "joy," but (Matthew's account) "when tribulation or persecution ariseth because of the word, by and by he is offended." These are they who have no root in themselves, and consequently (as Luke's account informs us) "for a while believe, and in time of temptation fall away." Theirs is naught but a temporary and evanescent faith, as we much fear is the case with the great majority of the "converts" from special missions and "evangelistic campaigns."

The third, or thorny-ground, hearer is the most difficult to identify, but the Lord has graciously supplied fuller help on this point by entering into more detail in His explanations of what the "thorns" signify. All three accounts tell us that they "grew up," which implies that no effort was made to check them; and all three accounts show that they "choked" the seed or hindered the Word. Matthew's record defines the thorns as "the care of this world, and the deceitfulness of riches." Mark adds "and the lust of other things entering in." While Luke mentions also "the pleasures of this life." Thus we are taught that there is quite a variety of things which hinder any fruit being brought to perfection — against each of which we need to be much on our prayerful guard. The good-ground hearer is the one who "understandeth" the Word (Matt. 13:23), for unless its sense be perceived it profits us nothing — probably an experiential acquaintance therewith is also included. Mark 4 mentions the "receiving" of it (cf. James 1:21), while Luke 8 describes this hearer as receiving the Word "in an honest and good heart," which is one that hates all pretence and loves the Truth for itself, making application of the Word to his own case and judging himself by it; "keeps it," cherishes and meditates upon it, heeds and obeys it; and "brings forth fruit with patience."

In a preceding chapter we called attention to Matthew 7:24-27, as an example of the importance of ascertaining the scope of a passage. Let us now point out the need for *comparing it* with the parallel passage in Luke 6:47-49. In it the hearers of the Word are likened unto wise and foolish builders. The former built his house on the foundation of God's Word. The building is the character developed thereby and the hope cherished. The storm which beat upon the house is the trial or testing to which it is subjected. Luke alone begins his account by saying the wise man came to Christ — to learn of Him. His wisdom appeared in the trouble he took and the pains he went to in order to find a secure base on the rock. Luke's account adds that he "digged deep," which tells of his earnestness and care, and signifies spiritually that he searched the Scriptures closely and diligently examined his heart and profession — that digging deep is in designed contrast with the "no depth of earth" (Mark 4:5) of the stony-ground hearer. Luke alone uses the word "vehemently" to describe the violence of the storm by which it was tested: his profession survived the assaults of the world, the flesh and the devil, and the scrutiny of God at the moment of death; which proves he was a *doer* of the Word and not a hearer only (James 1:22). Useless is the confession of the lips unless it be confirmed by the life.

The comparing of Scripture with Scripture is valuable for the purpose of *harmonization* or preserving the balance of Truth, thus preventing our becoming lopsided. An illustration of this is found in connection with what is termed "the great commission," a threefold record of which, with notable variations, is given in the last chapter of each of the Synoptic Gospels. In order to obtain a right or full knowledge of the complete charge Christ there gave unto His servants, instead of confining our attention to only one or two of them — as is now so often the case — the three accounts of it need to be brought together. Luke 24:47, shows it is just as much the minister's duty "that *repentance* and remission of sins should be preached in His name" as it is to bid sinners "believe on Him"; and Matthew 28:19, 20, makes it clear that it devolves as much upon him to baptize those who believe and then to teach them to observe all things whatsoever He commanded as to "preach the gospel to every creature." Quality is even more important than quantity! One of the chief reasons why so few of the Christian churches in heathen lands are self-supporting is that missionaries have too often failed in thoroughly indoctrinating and building up their converts, leaving them in an infantile state and going elsewhere seeking to evangelize more of their fellows.

Failure to heed this important principle lies at the foundation of much of the defective evangelism of our day, wherein the lost are informed that the only thing necessary for their salvation is to "believe in the Lord Jesus Christ." Other passages show that repentance is equally essential: "Repent ye, and believe the gospel" (Mark 1:15), "Repentance toward God, and faith toward our Lord Jesus Christ" (Acts 20:21). It is important to note that wherever the two are mentioned repentance always comes *first*, for in the very nature of the case it is impossible for an impenitent heart to believe savingly (Matt. 21:32). Repentance is a realization of my blameworthiness in being a rebel against God, a taking sides with Him and condemning myself. It expresses itself in bitter sorrow for and hatred of sin. It results in an acknowledgment of my offenses and the heart abandonment of my idols (Prov. 28:13), a throwing down the weapons of my warfare, a forsaking of my evil ways (Isa. 55:7). In some passages, like Luke 13:3; Acts 2:38; 3:19, repentance alone is mentioned. In John 3:15; Romans 1:16; 10:4, only "believing" is specified. Why is this? Because the Scriptures are not written like lawyers draw up documents, wherein terms are wearily repeated and multiplied. Each verse must be interpreted in the light of Scripture as a whole: thus where "repentance" only is mentioned believing is implied; and where "believing" alone is found repentance is presupposed.

7. *Briefer statements are to be interpreted by fuller ones.* It is an invariable rule of exegesis that when anything is set out more fully or clearly by one writer than another the latter is always to be expounded by the former, and the same applies to two statements by the same speaker or writer. Particularly is this the case with the first three Gospels: parallel passages should be consulted, and the shorter one interpreted in the light of the longer one. Thus, when Peter asked Christ, "How often shall my brother sin against me, and I forgive him? till seven times?" and our Lord answered "Until seventy times seven" (Matt. 18:

21, 22) it must not be taken to signify that a Christian is to condone wrongs and exercise grace at the expense of righteousness; for He had just previously said, "If thy brother shall trespass against thee, go and tell him his fault between thee and him alone: if he shall hear [heed] thee, thou hast gained thy brother" (v. 15). No, rather must Christ's language in Matthew 18:22, be explained by His amplified declaration in Luke 17:3, 4 — "If thy brother trespass against thee, rebuke him; and if he repent, forgive him. And if he trespass against thee seven times in a day, and seven times in a day turn again to thee, saying, I *repent*; thou shalt forgive him": God Himself does not forgive us until we repent (Acts 2:38; 3:19)! If a brother repents not, no malice is to be harbored against him; yet he is not to be treated as though no offense had been committed.

Much harm has been done by some who, without qualification, pressed our Lord's words in Mark 10:11, "Whosoever shall put away his wife, and marry another, committeth adultery against her," thereby subjecting the innocent party to the same penalty as the guilty one. But that statement is to be interpreted in the light of the fuller one in Matthew 5:32, "Whosoever shall put away his wife, *saving* for the cause of fornication, causeth her to commit adultery: and whosoever shall marry her that is divorced [for any other cause] committeth adultery" — repeated by Christ in Matthew 19:9. In those words the sole Legislator for His people propounded a general rule: "*Whosoever* putteth away his wife causeth her to commit adultery," and then He put in an *exception,* namely that where adultery has taken place he *may* put away, and he *may* marry again. As Christ there teaches the lawfulness of divorce on the ground of marital infidelity, so He teaches that it is lawful for the innocent one to marry again after such a divorce, without contracting guilt. The violation of the marriage vows severs the marriage bond, and the one who kept them is, after divorce is obtained, free to marry again.

8

8. THE need of *collecting and collating* all passages dealing with the same subject, where cognate terms or different expressions are used. This is essential if the expositor is to be preserved from erroneous conceptions thereof, and in order for him to obtain the full mind of the Spirit thereon. Take as a simple example those well-known words, "Ask, and it shall be given you" (Matt. 7:7). Few texts have been more grievously perverted than that one. Many have regarded it as a sort of blank cheque, which anybody — no matter what his state of soul or manner of walk — may fill in just as he pleases, and that he has but to present the same at the throne of grace and God stands pledged to honor it. Such a travesty of the Truth would not deserve refutation were it not now being trumpeted so loudly in some quarters. James 4:3, expressly states of some, "Ye ask, and receive not, because ye ask amiss": some who "ask" do *not* receive! And why? Because theirs is but a carnal asking — "that ye may consume it upon your own lusts" — and therefore a holy God denies them.

Asking God in prayer is one thing; asking becomingly, rightly, acceptably and effectually is quite another. If we would ascertain *how* the latter is to be done, the Scriptures must be searched for the answer. Thus, in order to ensure a Divine hearing, we must approach God through the Mediator: "Whatsoever ye shall ask the Father in My name, He will give it you" (John 16:23). But to ask the Father in His name signifies very much more than just uttering the words "grant it for Christ's sake." Among other things it signifies asking in Christ's person, as identified with and united to Him; asking for that which accords with His perfections and will be for His glory; asking for that which *He* would were He in our place. Again, we must ask in faith (Mark 11:24), for God will place no premium upon unbelief. Said Christ to His disciples, "If ye abide in Me, and My words abide in you, ye shall ask what ye will, and it shall be done unto you" (John 15:7), where two further conditions are stipulated. In order to receive we must ask according to God's will (I John 5:14) as made known in His Word. What a deplorable misuse has been made of Matthew 7:7, through failure to interpret it in the light of collateral passages!

Another example of failure at this point is the frequent use made of Galatians 6:15, "For in Christ Jesus neither circumcision availeth any thing, nor uncircumcision, but a new creature" (or "new creation"). It is most proper and pertinent to use that verse when showing that neither the ceremonial ordinances of Judaism nor the baptism and Lord's supper of Christianity are of any worth in rendering us meet for the inheritance of the saints in light. So too, though much less frequently, we are reminded that, "For in Christ Jesus neither circumcision availeth any thing, nor uncircumcision; but faith which worketh by love" (Gal. 5:6), that is out of gratitude to God for His unspeakable Gift, and not from legal motives — only for what they may obtain. But how very rarely does the pulpit quote "Circumcision is nothing, and uncircumcision is nothing, but the keeping of the commandments of God" (I Cor. 7:19) — that which respects our submission to the Divine authority, our walking in subjection to God's will, is omitted. It is only by placing these three verses side by side that we obtain a balanced view. We are not vitally united to Christ unless we have been born again; we are not born again unless we possess a faith that works by love; and we have not this saving faith unless it be evidenced by a keeping of God's commandments.

It is the duty of the expositor to gather together the various descriptions and exemplifications given in Scripture of any particular thing, rather than to frame a formal definition of its nature, for it is in this way that the Holy Spirit has taught us to conceive of it. Take the simple *act of saving faith*, and observe the numerous and quite different expressions used to depict it. It is portrayed as believing on the Lord Jesus Christ (Acts 16:31), or the reposing of the soul's confidence in Him. As a coming to Him (Matt. 11:28), which implies the forsaking of all that is opposed to Him. As a receiving of Him (John 1:12), as He is freely offered to sinners in the Gospel. As a fleeing to Him for refuge (Heb. 6:18), as the manslayer sought asylum in one of the cities provided for that purpose (Num. 35:6). As a looking unto Him (Isa. 45:22), as the bitten Israelites unto the serpent upon the pole (Num. 21:9). As an acceptance of God's testimony, and thereby setting to our seal that He is true (John 3:33). As the entering of a gate (Matt. 7:13) or door (John 10:9). As an act of complete surrender or giving of ourselves to the Lord (II Cor. 8:5), as a woman does when she marries a man.

The act of saving faith is also set forth as a calling upon the Lord (Rom. 10:13), as did sinking Peter (Matt. 14:30) and the dying thief. As a trusting in Christ (Eph. 1:13) as the great Physician, counting upon His sufficiency to heal our desperate diseases. As a resting in the Lord (Ps. 37:7) as on a sure foundation (Isa. 28:16). As an act of appropriation or eating (John 6:51) to satisfy an aching void within. As a committal (II Tim. 1:12): as a man deposits his money in a bank for safe custody, so we are to put our souls into the hands of Christ for time and eternity (cf. Luke 23:46). As faith in His blood (Rom. 3:25). As a belief of the Truth (II Thess. 2:13). As an act of obedience unto God's holy commandment (II Peter 2:21) in complying with the terms of the Gospel (Rom. 10:16). As a loving of the Lord Jesus Christ (I Cor. 16:22). As a turning unto the Lord (Acts 11:21) — which implies a turning from the world. As a receiving of the witness of God (I John 5:9, 10) as an all sufficient ground of assurance, without the evidence of feeling or anything else. As a taking of the water of life (Rev. 22:17). Most of these twenty expressions are figurative, and therefore better fitted than any formal definition to convey to our minds a more vivid concept of the act and to preserve from a one-sided view of it.

Much harm has been done by incompetent "novices" when treating of the subject of *regeneration*, by confining themselves to a single term — "born again." This is only one of many figures used in Scripture to describe that miracle of grace which is wrought in the soul when he passes from death unto life and is brought out of darkness into God's marvellous light. It is termed a new birth because a Divine life is communicated and there is the commencement of a new experience. But it is also likened to a spiritual resurrection, which presents a very different line of thought, and to a "renewing" (Col. 3:10), which imports a change in the original individual. It is the person who is Divinely quickened and not merely a "nature" which is begotten of God: "Ye must be born again" (John 3:7), not merely something *in you* must be; "*he* is born of God" (I John 3:9). The same person who was spiritually dead — his whole being alienated from God — is then made alive: his whole being reconciled to Him. This must be so, otherwise there would be no preservation of the *identity* of the individual. It is a new birth of the individual himself, and not of something in him. The nature is never changed, but the person is — relatively not absolutely.

If we limit ourselves to the figure of the new birth when considering the great change wrought in one whom God saves, not only will a very inadequate concept of the same be obtained, but a thoroughly erroneous one. In other passages it is spoken of as an illuminating of the mind (Acts 26:13), a searching and convicting of the conscience (Rom. 7:9), a renovating of the heart (Ezek. 11:19), a subduing of the will (Ps. 110: 3), a bringing of our thoughts into subjection to Christ (II Cor. 10:5), a writing of God's Law on the heart (Heb. 8:10). In some passages something is said to be removed from the individual (Deut. 30:6; Ezek. 36: 26) — the love of sin, enmity against God; while in others something is communicated (Rom. 5:5; I John 5:20). The figures of creation (Eph. 2:10), renewing (Titus 3:5) and resurrection (I John 3:14) are also employed. In some passages this miracle appears to be a completed thing (I Cor. 6:11; Col. 1:12), in others as a process yet going on (II Cor. 3:18; Phil. 1:16). Though the work of grace be one, yet it is many-sided. Its subject is a composite creature and his salvation affects every part of his complex being.

Physical birth is the bringing into this world of a creature, a complete personality, which before conception had no existence whatever. But the one regenerated by God had a complete personality *before* he was born again. Regeneration is not the creation of an individual which hitherto existed not, but the spiritualizing of one who already exists — the renewing and renovating of one whom sin has unfitted for communion with God, by bestowing upon him that which gives a new bias to all his faculties. Beware of regarding the Christian as made up of two distinct and diverse personalities. Responsibility attaches to the individual and not to his "nature" or "natures." While both sin and grace indwell the saint, God holds him accountable to resist and subdue the one and yield to and be regulated by the other. The fact that this miracle of grace is also likened to a resurrection (John 5:25) should prevent us forming a one-sided idea of what is imported by the new birth and "the new creature," and from pressing some analogies from natural birth which other figurative expressions *disallow*. The great inward change is also likened to a Divine "begetting" (I Peter 1:3), because the image of the Begetter is then stamped upon the soul. As the first Adam begat a son in his own image (Gen. 5:3), so the last Adam has an "image" (Rom. 8:29) to convey to His sons (Eph. 4:24).

What has been pointed out above applies with equal force to the subject of *mortification* (Col. 3:5). That essential Christian duty is set forth in the Scriptures under a great variety of figurative expressions, and it is most needful that we take pains to collect and compare them if we are to be preserved from faulty views of what God requires from His people on this important matter of resisting and overcoming evil. It is spoken of as a circumcizing of the heart (Deut. 11:16), a plucking out of the right eye and cutting off of the right hand (Matt. 5:29, 30), which tells of its painfulness. It is a denying of self and taking up of the cross (Matt. 16:24). It is a casting off of the works of darkness (Rom. 13:12), a putting off of the old man (Eph. 4:22), a laying apart of all filthiness and superfluity of naughtiness (James 1:21) — each of which is necessary *before* we can put on the armor of light or the new man, or receive with meekness the ingrafted Word, for we have to cease doing evil ere we can do well (Isa. 1:16, 17). It is a making no provision for the flesh (Rom. 13:14), a keeping under the body, i.e., of sin (Rom. 6:6; Col. 2:11) and bringing it into subjection (I Cor. 9:27), a cleansing of ourselves from all filthiness of the flesh and spirit (II Cor. 7:1), and abstinence from all appearance of evil (I Thess. 5:22), a laying aside of every weight (Heb. 12:1).

9. Equally necessary is it *not to sever* what God has joined together. By nature all of us are prone to run to extremes, particularly so those with a philosophical turn of mind, who, seeking for unity of thought, are in great danger of *forcing* a unity into the sphere of their limited knowledge. To do this, they are very apt to sacrifice one side or element of the Truth for another. I may be quite clear and logical at the expense of being superficial and half-orbed. A most solemn warning against this danger was supplied by the Jews in connection with their interpretation of the Messianic prophecies, by dwelling exclusively upon those which announced the glories of Christ and neglecting those which foretold His sufferings: so that even the apostles themselves were evilly affected thereby, and rebuked by Christ for such folly (Luke 24:25, 26). It is at this very point that the people of God, and particularly His ministers, need to be much on their guard. Truth is twofold (Heb. 4:12): every doctrine has its corresponding and supplementary element, every privilege its implied obligation. Those two sides of the Truth do not cross each other, but run parallel with one another: they are not contradictory but complementary, and both must be held fast by us if we are to be kept from serious error.

Thus we must never allow the grand truth of God's sovereignty to crowd out the fact of human responsibility. The will of the Almighty is indeed invincible, but that does not mean that we are nothing better than inanimate puppets. No, we are moral agents as well as rational creatures, and throughout are dealt with by God as such. "It must needs be that offenses come," said Christ, but He at once added, "woe to that man by whom the offense cometh" (Matt. 18:7). There the two things are joined together: the infallible certainty of the Divine decrees, the culpability and criminality of the human agent. The same inseparable conjunction appears again in that statement concerning the death of Christ: "Him, being delivered by the determinate counsel and foreknowledge of God, ye have taken, and by *wicked* hands have crucified and slain" (Acts 2:23). Again, our zeal for the doctrine of election must not suffer us to ignore the necessity of using means. They who reason, If I be elected, I shall be saved whether or not I repent and trust in Christ, are fatally deceiving themselves: "chosen you to salvation *through* sanctification of the Spirit and belief of the truth" (II Thess. 2:13) is proof. None are ever saved until they believe (Luke 8:12; Heb. 10:39), and therefore all are to be exhorted to do so.

Particular redemption (Christ making atonement for the sins of His own people only) must not prevent His servants from preaching the Gospel to every creature and announcing that there is a Saviour for every sinner out of hell who appropriates Him for his own. Sunder not the two halves of John 6:37: all that the Father gives Christ shall come to Him, albeit the individual must *seek Him* (Isa. 55:6; Jer. 29:13). Nor does the inability of the natural man annul his accountability, for though no man can come to Christ except the Father draw him (John 6:44), his refusal to come is highly blameworthy (Prov. 1:24-31; John 5:40). Nor is a divided Christ to be presented to sinners for their acceptance. It is a delusion to imagine that His priestly sacrifice may be received while His kingly rule is refused, that His blood will save me though I despise His government. Christ is both "Lord and Saviour" and in that unalterable order (II Peter 1:11; 3:2, 18), for we must throw down the weapons of our warfare against Him and take His yoke upon us in order to find rest unto our souls. Thus repentance and faith are equally necessary (Mark 1:15; Acts 20:21).

While justification and sanctification are to be sharply distinguished, nevertheless they must not be divorced (I Cor. 1:30; 6:11). "Christ never comes into the soul unattended. He brings the Holy Spirit with Him, and the Spirit His train of gifts and graces. Christ comes with a blessing in each hand: forgiveness in one, holiness in the other" (Thos. Adams, 1650). Yet how rarely is Ephesians 2:8, 9, completed by the quoting of verse 10! Again, the twin truths of Divine preservation and Christian perseverance must not be parted, for the former is accomplished via the latter and not without it. We are indeed "kept by the power of God," yet "through faith" (I Peter 1:5), and if in I John 2:27, the apostle assured the saints "ye *shall* abide in Him," in the very next verse he called on them *to* "abide in Him"; as Paul also bade such work out their own salvation with fear and trembling, and then added "For it is God which worketh in you both to will and to do of His good pleasure" (Phil. 2:13). Balaam wished to die the death of the righteous, but was not willing to live the life of one. Means and ends are not to be separated: we shall never reach heaven unless we continue in the only way (the "narrow" one) which leads thereto.

9

10. *The simple negative* often implies, conversely, the positive. This is a very simple canon of exegesis, yet one to which the attention of the young student needs to be called. A negative statement is, of course, one where something is denied or where the absence of its opposite is supposed. In common speech the reverse of a negative usually holds good, as when we declare, "I hope it will not rain today," it is the same as saying, "I trust it will remain fine." That this rule obtains in Scripture is clear from the numerous instances where the antithesis is stated. "Thou wilt not suffer Thine Holy One to see corruption" is explained in "Thou wilt show Me the path of life (Ps. 16:10, 11). "I have not refrained My lips, O Lord, Thou knowest. I have not hid Thy righteousness within My heart," and then the positive side at once follows: "I have declared Thy faithfulness and Thy salvation" (Ps. 40:9, 10). "Wherefore putting away lying, speak every man truth with his neighbor . . . Let him that stole steal no more: but rather let him labor," (Eph. 4:25, 28). Many other examples might be given, but these are sufficient to establish the rule we are here treating of.

Now the Holy Spirit has by no means always formally drawn the antithesis, but rather has in many instances — that we might exercise our minds upon His Word — left *us* to do so. Thus, "A bruised reed shall He not break, and smoking flax shall He not quench" (Matt. 12:20) signifies that He will tenderly care for and nourish the same. "The scripture cannot be broken" (John 10:35) is the equivalent of, It must be, it most certainly will be, fulfilled. "Without Me ye can do nothing" (John 15: 5) implies that in union and communion with Him we "*can* do all things" (Phil. 4:13) — incidentally note how the former serves to define the latter: it is not that I shall then be able to perform miracles, but fitted to bring forth *fruit!* "Be not unequally yoked together with unbelievers" (II Cor. 6:14) has the force of "Come out from among them and be ye separate," as verse 17 shows. "Let us not be desirous of vain glory" (Gal. 5:26) imports Be lowly in mind and esteem others better than yourself (Phil. 2:3). "These things write I unto you, that ye sin not" (I John 2: 1) equals My design is to inculcate and promote the practice of holiness, as all that follows clearly shows.

Negative commandments enjoin the opposite good: "Thou shalt not take the name of the Lord thy God in vain" (Exod. 20:7) implies that we are to hold His name in the utmost reverence and hallow it in our hearts. Negative threatenings are tacit affirmations: "The Lord will not hold him guiltless that taketh His name in vain": rather will He condemn and punish him. Negative promises contain positive assurances: "A broken and contrite heart O God, Thou wilt not despise" (Ps. 51:17) means that such a heart is acceptable to Him. "No good thing will He withhold from them that walk uprightly" (Ps. 84:11) is tantamount to saying that everything which is truly good for such will certainly be bestowed upon them. Negative conclusions involve their opposites: "The father of the fool hath no joy" (Prov. 17:21) purports that he will suffer much sorrow and anguish because of him — oh, that wayward children would make conscience of the grief which they occasion their parents. "To have respect of persons is not good" (Prov. 28:21), but evil. Negative statements carry with them strong assertives: "Yea, surely God will not do wickedly, neither will the Almighty pervert judgment" (Job 34:12): rather will He act holily and govern righteously.

11. In sharp contrast with the above, it should be pointed out that in many cases statements put in the *interrogative form* have the force of an emphatic negative. This is another simple rule which all expositors should keep in mind. "Canst thou by searching find out God? canst thou find out the Almighty unto perfection?" (Job 11:7) — indeed no. "Which of you by taking thought can add one cubit unto his stature?" (Matt. 6:27) — none can do so by any such means. "For what is a man profited, if he shall gain the whole world, and lose his own soul?" (Matt. 16:26) — nothing whatever, nay, he is immeasurably, worse off. "Ye generation of vipers, how can ye escape the damnation of hell?" (Matt. 23:33) — they cannot. "How can ye believe, which receive honor one of another, and seek not the honor that cometh from God only?" (John 5:44) — such is morally impossible. "How shall they believe in Him of whom they have not heard?" (Rom. 10:14) — they will not. On the other hand, the question of Matthew 6:30, is a strong affirmation; while that of Matthew 6:28, is a prohibition.

12. *The right use of reason* in connection with the things of God. This is another rule of exegesis which is of considerable importance, yet one that requires to be used with holy care and caution, and by one of mature judgment and thorough acquaintance with the Word. For that reason it is not to be employed by the novice or inexperienced. The Christian, like the non-Christian, is endowed with rationality, and the sanctified exercise thereof certainly has its most fitting sphere in the realm of spiritual things. Before considering the application of reason to the expounding of the Truth, let us point out its more general province. Two examples thereof may be selected from the teaching of our Lord. "Wherefore, if God so clothe the grass of the field, which today is, and tomorrow is cast into the oven, shall He not much more clothe you, O ye of little faith?" (Matt. 6:30). Here we find Christ demonstrating, by a simple process of logic, the utter unreasonableness of distrustful anxiety in connection with the supply of temporal necessities. His argument is drawn from the consideration of Divine providence. If God cares for the field, much more will He for His dear people: He *evidences* His care for the field by clothing it with grass, *therefore* much more will He provide clothing for us.

If ye then, being evil, know how to give good gifts unto your children, how much more shall your Father which is in heaven give good things to them that ask Him?" (Matt. 7:11). Here again the Lord shows us how this faculty is to be employed by a process of holy reasoning. He was speaking on the subject of prayer, and presented an argument for assuring His disciples of their being heard at the throne of grace. The argument is based on a comparison of inequalities and the reason drawn from the less to the greater. It may be framed thus: If earthly parents, though sinful, are inclined to listen to the appeals of their little ones, most certainly our heavenly Father will not close His ears to the cries of His children: natural parents *do,* in fact, respond to and grant the requests of their little one, *therfore* much more will our Father deal graciously and generously with His. It is said of Abraham that he accounted or reckoned thus within himself: There is nothing impossible with God. Likewise the apostle, "For I reckon [convince myself by logical reasoning] that the sufferings of this present time are not worthy to be compared with the glory which shall be revealed in us" (Rom. 8:18). Other illustrations of Paul's inspired reasoning are found in Romans 5:9, 10; 8:31, 32. In all of these instances we are taught the legitimacy and right use of reasoning.

The Lord Jesus often argued, both with His disciples and with His adversaries, as with rational men, according to the principles of sound reasoning He did so from prophecy and the conformity of the event to the prediction (Luke 24:25, 26; John 5:39, 46). He did so from the miracles which He performed (John 10:25, 37, 38; 14:10, 11) as being incontrovertible evidence that He was sent of God, and reproved His despisers for failing to identify Him as the Messiah. His "Ye hypocrites, ye can discern the face of the sky and of the earth; but how is it that ye do not discern this time? Yea, and why even of yourselves judge ye not what is right?" (Luke 12:56, 57) was a direct and scathing rebuke because — on its lowest ground — they had failed to use properly their reasoning powers, as Nicodemus *did*: "We know that Thou art a teacher come from God: for no man can do these miracles that Thou doest, except God be with him" (John 3:2). So, too, the apostle when exhorting believers to flee from idolatry added: "I speak as to wise men; *judge ye what I say*" (I Cor. 10:15).

In his masterly exposition of Hebrews 4:3, Owen pointed out that the apostle's argument there rested upon the logical rule that "unto immediate contraries contrary attributes may certainly be ascribed, so that he who affirms the one at the same time denies the other; and on the contrary, he that denies the one affirms the other. He that saith it is day, doth as really say it is not night, as if he had used those formal words." His whole design in 4:1-11, was to demonstrate by various testimonies and examples that unbelief cuts off from the rest of God, whereas faith gives an entrance thereinto. In verse 3 he affirms, "For we which have believed do enter into rest," in substantiation of which he adds, "as He said, As I have sworn in my wrath, if they shall enter into My rest." There the apostle again quoted from Psalm 95 (see Heb. 3:7, 11, 15, 18). From the sad experience of Israel's failure to enter into God's rest because of their unbelief and disobedience Paul drew the obvious and inescapable conclusion that *believers* "*do* enter" therein.

We repeat, it is only by that principle of logic that the apostle's argument in Hebrews 4:3, can be understood. If any of our readers be inclined to take issue with that statement, then we would respectfully urge them to turn to and carefully ponder that verse, and see if they can perceive *how* the proof-text cited supplies any confirmation of the proposition laid down in its opening clause. From that exposition Owen pointed out, "And here by the way we may take notice of the *use of reason,* or logical deductions, in the proposing, handling and confirming of sacred supernatural truths and articles of faith. For the validity of the apostle's proof in this place depends upon the certainty of the logical maxim before mentioned, the consideration of which removes the whole difficulty. And to deny this liberty of deducing consequences, or one thing from another, according to the just rules of ratiocination, is quite to take away the use of the Scripture, and to banish reason from those things wherein it ought to be principally employed."

In Hebrews 8:13, is found another and yet much simpler example of reasoning upon Scripture. "In that He saith, A *new* covenant, He hath made the first *old.* Now that which decayeth and waxeth old is ready to vanish away." The apostle's design in this epistle was to exhibit the immeasurable superiority of Christianity over Judaism, and exhort Hebrew believers to cleave steadfastly unto Christ, the true light and substance, and not to return to the shadows and symbols of a system which had then served its purpose. Among other reasons, he had appealed to the promise of a "new covenant" made by Jehovah in Jeremiah 31:31-34. This he had cited in Hebrews 8:8-12, and then he *drew a logical inference* from the word "new" — God's calling this better economy a new one clearly implied that the previous one had become obsolete: just as the Psalmist (102:25, 26), when affirming that the present earth and heavens would perish, added as proof that they should "wax old like a garment." Thus the declaration made in Hebrews 8:13, is (by way of logical deduction) adduced as a proof of the proposition stated in 8:7, "For if that first covenant had been faultless, then should no place have been sought for the second."

In Ephesians 4:8, Paul quotes from Psalm 68:18, and then shows us how we are to make a right use of reason or to exercise the intellectual and moral faculties: "Now that He ascended, what is it but that He also descended?": the exaltation of Christ *presupposed* a previous humiliation. Again, "Do you think that the scripture saith in vain, The spirit that dwelleth in us lusteth to envy?" (James 4:5). But as Thomas Manton pointed out in his exposition of that verse, such a statement is nowhere found in the Bible in those particular terms, adding "The Scripture 'saith' that which may be *inferred* from the scope of it by just consequence. Immediate inferences are as valid as express words. Christ proved the resurrection not by direct testimony, but by argument (Matt. 22:32). What the Scripture doth *import* therefore by good consequence should be received as if it were expressed." Still another of the apostles had recourse to reasoning when he said, "If we receive the witness of men, the witness of God is greater" (I John 5:9), and infinitely more dependable; hence the excuselessness of those who reject it.

Those who are familiar with the writings of Augustine and Calvin will have observed how frequently they drew the inference that whatever be freely *bestowed* by God is something of which fallen man, considered in himself, *is destitute*. It is an obvious deduction of reason, and a sure canon of exegesis, which is of simple and universal application, that everything which is graciously supplied in and by Christ is wanting in our natural condition. Thus, every verse which speaks of eternal life as a Divine gift, or which makes promise of it to those who believe, necessarily presupposes that we are without it, and therefore spiritually dead. So, too, the Christian's receiving of the Holy Spirit (Acts 2:38; Gal. 3:2; 4:6) takes it for granted that in their unregenerate condition they were without Him, having forfeited His indwelling presence by sin; the same being graciously restored to us by the mediation of Christ (John 7:39; Gal. 3:14). As the result of the fall, the Holy Spirit was — in the exercise of Divine justice — withdrawn from the human heart, and in consequence it was left not only without a Divine inhabitant, but a prey of all those influences — natural, worldly, satanic — which, in the absence of the Holy Spirit, inevitably draw the affections away from God; but at regeneration the Spirit is again given (Ezek. 34:27).

While the faculty of reason is vastly superior to our bodily senses (distinguishing man from and elevating him above the animals), it is greatly inferior to faith (the gift of God to His people), and that, in turn, to the Holy Spirit — upon whom we are dependent for the directing of the one and the strengthening of the other. There is much confusion of mind and not a little wrong thinking on the part of the saints concerning the place and extent which reason may and should have in connection with the Scriptures. Assuredly God has not subordinated His word to our reason for us to accept only what commends itself to our judgment. Nevertheless, He has furnished His people with this faculty, and though insufficient of itself it is a valuable aid in the understanding of Truth. While reason is not be be made the measurer of our belief, yet it is to be used as the handmaid of faith, by comparing passage with passage, deducing inferences and drawing consequences according to the legitimate laws of logic. Never is the faculty of reason so worthily employed as in endeavoring to understand Holy Writ. If on the one hand we are forbidden to lean unto our own understanding (Prov. 3:5), on the other we are exhorted to apply our hearts to understanding (Prov. 2:2).

God has supplied us with an unerring standard by which we may *test* every exercise of our reason upon His Word, namely the Analogy of Faith. And it is *there* that we have a sure safeguard against the wrong use of this faculty. Though it be true that very often more is implied by the words of Scripture than is actually expressed, yet reason is not a law unto itself to make any supplement it pleases. Any deduction we make, however logical it seems, any consequence we draw, no matter how plausible it be, is *erroneous* if it be *repugnant* to other passages. For example, when we read "Be ye therefore perfct, even as your Father which is in heaven is perfect" (Matt. 5:48), we may conclude that sinless perfection is attainable in this life, but if we do so we err, as Philippians 3:12, and I John 1:8, show. Again, should I draw the inference from Christ's words "no man can come to Me, except the Father which hath sent Me draw him" (John 6:44) that therefore I am in no wise responsible *to come* unto Him, that my inability excuses me, then I certainly err, as John 5:40, and other passages make clear.

10

It is of first importance that the expositor should constantly bear in mind that not only are the substance and the sentiments expressed in Holy Writ of Divine origin, but that the whole of its contents are verbally inspired. Its own affirmations lay considerable emphasis upon that fact. Said holy Job, "I have esteemed *the words* of His mouth more than my necessary food" (23:12): he not only venerated God's Word in its entirety, but highly prized each syllable in it. "The *words* of the Lord are pure words: as silver tried in a furnace of earth, purified seven times" (Ps. 12:6). We believe that is more than a general statement concerning the preciousness, purity and permanence of what proceeds out of the mouth of Jehovah, for it is to be duly noted that the Divine utterances are not simply likened to silver tried in a furnace, but to "a furnace *of earth.*" Though the Holy Spirit has employed the vernacular of earth, yet He has purged what He uses from all human dross, giving some of His terms an entirely different force from their human original, investing many of them with a higher meaning, and applying all with spiritual perfection — as the "purified *seven* times" purports. Thus, "every word of God is pure" (Prov. 30:5).

The Lord Jesus repeatedly laid stress on this aspect of the Truth. When making known to His disciples the fundamental requirements of their receiving answers to prayer, He said, "If ye abide in Me [maintain a spirit of constant dependence upon and remain in communion with Him], and My *words* abide in you [forming your thoughts and regulaing your desires], ye shall ask what ye will, and it shall be done unto you" (John 15:7) — for in such cases they would request only that which would be for God's glory and their own real good. Again, He declared, "the *words* that I speak unto you, they are spirit, and they are life" (John 6:63). God's Word then is made up of words, and each one in it is selected by Divine wisdom and positioned with unerring precision. It therefore behoves us to spare no pains in seeking to ascertain the exact meaning of each of its terms and most diligently to scrutinize the exact order in which they are placed, for the right understanding of a passage turns first upon our obtaining a correct understanding of its language. That should be so obvious as to require no argument, yet it is surprising how often that elementary principle is ignored and contravened.

Before stating several more rules which should direct the expositor, particularly those which relate more directly to the interpretation of words and phrases, let us mention several warnings which need to be heeded. First, do not assume at the outset that all is plain and intelligible to you, for often the words of Scripture are used in a different and higher sense than they are in common speech. Thus it is not sufficient to be acquainted with their dictionary meaning: rather do we have to ascertain how they are used by the Holy Spirit. For example, "hope" signifies very much more in the Word of God than it does on the lips of men. Second, do not jump to the conclusion that you have arrived at the meaning of a term because its force is quite obvious in one or two passages, for you are not in a position to frame a definition until you have weighed *every* occurrence of it. That demands much toil and patience, yet such are necessary if we are to be preserved from erroneous ideas. Third, do not conclude that any term employed by the Spirit has one uniform signification, for that is far from being the case. The force of these cautions will be made the more apparent in the paragraphs that follow.

13. *The limitation of general statements.* General statements are frequently to be limited, both in themselves and their application. Many examples of this principle occur in the book of Proverbs, and obviously so, for a proverb or maxim is a broad principle expressed in a brief form, a moral truth set forth in condensed and universal language. Thus, "He that is surety for a stranger shall smart for it; and he that hateth suretiship is sure" (11:15) enunciates the general rule, yet there are exceptions thereto. "Children's children are the crown of old men; and the glory of children are their fathers" (17:6), though that is far from being the case in every instance. "Whoso findeth a wife findeth a good thing, and obtaineth favor of the Lord" (18:22), as many a man — the writer included — has discovered; yet the experience of not a few has been quite to the contrary. "Foolishness is bound up in the heart of a child; but the rod of correction shall drive it from him" (22:15), yet God reserves to Himself the sovereign right to make that good to whom He pleases — where He blesses not this means, the child is hardened in his perversity. "Seest thou a man diligent in his business? he shall stand before kings" (22:29), though sometimes the most industrious meet with little material success.

General statements must be qualified if to interpret them in an unlimited sense clashes with other verses. A case in point is our Lord's prohibition, "Judge not, that ye be not judged" (Matt. 7:1), for if that injunction be taken without any restriction it would flatly contradict His precept, "judge righteous judgment" (John 7:24); yet how often is this precept hurled at the heads of those performing a Christian duty. The capacity to weigh or judge, to form an estimate and opinion, is one of the most valuable of our faculties, and the right use of it one of our most important tasks. It is very necessary that we have our senses "exercised to discern [Greek "thoroughly judge"] both good and evil" (Heb. 5:14) if we are not to be deceived by appearances and taken in by every oily-mouthed impostor we encounter. Unless we form a judgment of what is true and false, how can we embrace the one and avoid the other? We are bidden to "beware of false prophets," but how can we do so unless we judge or carefully measure every preacher by the Word of God? We are prohibited from having fellowship with the unfruitful works of darkness, but that requires us to determine *which* are such. Christ was not here forbidding all judging of others, but was reprehending an officious or magisterial, a presumptuous, hypocritical, rash or hasty, unwarrantable, unfair, and unmerciful judgment. Much grace and wisdom is required by us to heed rightly this word of our Master's.

Another pertinent example is found in our Lord's "Swear not at all" (Matt. 5:34). In the section of the sermon on the mount in which those words occur, Christ was freeing the Divine commandments from the errors of the rabbis and Pharisees, enforcing their strictness and spirituality. In the instance now before us, the Jewish doctors had restricted the Mosaic statutes upon oaths to the simple prohibition against perjury, encouraging the habit of swearing by the creature and the taking of oaths lightly in ordinary conversation. In verses 34-37 our Lord inveighed against those corrupt traditions and practices. That He never intended His "swear not at all" to be taken absolutely is clear from His bidding men to swear by no creature, and from His reprehending all oaths in ordinary conversation. The general analogy of Scripture reveals the need for oaths on certain occasions. Abraham swore to Abimelech (Gen. 21:23, 24) and required his servant to take an oath (Gen. 24:8, 9); Jacob (Gen. 31:53) and Joseph (Gen. 47:31) each took one. Paul repeatedly confirmed his teaching by solemnly calling God for a witness (Rom. 9:1; II Cor. 1:23, etc.). Hebrews 6:16, indicates that oaths are both permissible and requisite.

There are many expressions used in the Scriptures indefinitely rather than specifically, and which are not to be understood without qualification. Some of them are more or less apparent, others can only be discovered by a comparison and study of other passages treating of the same subject. Thus, "the salvation of God is sent unto *the Gentiles*, and that they will hear it" (Acts 28:28, and cf. 11:18) did not signify that every one of them would do so. Similarly, "The glory of the Lord shall be revealed, and *all flesh* shall see it together" (Isa. 40:5) and "I will pour out My Spirit upon all flesh" (Acts 2:17) were simply announcements that the grace of God was to overflow the narrow bounds of Israel after the flesh. So too "the world" has a variety of meanings and is very rarely synonymous with all mankind. In such passages as John 7:4, and 12:19, only a very small part of its inhabitants were included. In Luke 2:1, the profane world is in view; in John 15:18, 19, the professing world, for it was the religious sections of Israel which hated Christ. In John 14:17, and 17:9, it is the non-elect who are referred to — compare "the world of the ungodly" (II Peter 2:5), whereas in John 1:29, and 6:33, it is the world of God's elect, who are all actually saved by Christ.

Another word which is used in the Bible with considerable latitude is "all," and very rarely is it found *without* limitation. "All things, whatsoever ye shall ask in prayer, believing, ye shall receive" (Matt. 21:22) obviously means whatsoever we ask that is according to God's will (I John 5:14). When the apostles said to Christ, "All seek for Thee" (Mark 1:37), that "all did marvel" at His miracles (Mark 5:20), and that "all the people came unto Him" in the temple (John 8:2), those expressions were far from signifying the sum total of the inhabitants of Palestine. When Luke tells his readers that he "had perfect understanding of all things from the very first" (1:3), and when we are informed that Christ foretold all things (Mark 13:23) unto His apostles, such language is not to be taken absolutely. In like manner such statements as "all glorified God for that which was done" (Acts 4:21), "this is the man, that teacheth all men every where against the people, and the law" (Acts 21:28), "thou shalt be His witness unto all men" (Acts 22:15), are to be regarded relatively. Consequently, in the light of those examples, when he deals with "He died for all" (II Cor. 5:15) and "gave Himself a ransom for all" (I Tim. 2:6), the expositor must ascertain from other Scriptures (such as Isa. 53:8; Matt. 1:21; Eph. 5:25) whether they mean all mankind or all who believe.

The same is true of the expression "every man" (see for instance, Mark 8:25; Luke 16:16; Rom. 12:3; and compare II Thess. 3:2; I Cor. 4:5). So too the words "all things." Neither "all things are clean unto you" (Luke 11:41) nor "all things are lawful unto me" (I Cor. 6:12) can be taken at face value, or many Scriptures would be contradicted. "I am made all things to all men" (I Cor. 9:22), must be explained by what immediately precedes. The "all things" of Rom. 8:28, has reference to "the sufferings of this present time," and the "all things" of 8:32, means the "all things that pertain unto life and godliness" (II Peter 1:3). The "times of restitution of all things" (Acts 3:21) is at once modified by the words immediately following: "which God hath spoken by the mouth of all His holy prophets since the world began," and most certainly none of them predicted the restoration of the Devil, and his angels to their pristine glory. "To reconcile all things unto Himself" (Col. 1:20) must not be understood to teach undiluted Universalism, or every passage affirming the eternal damnation of the Christless would be contradicted.

14. *Positive statements with a comparative force.* Many injunctions in Scripture are expressed in an absolute form, yet are to be understood relatively. This is evident from those examples which are there and thus explained. "Lay not up for yourselves treasures upon earth" (Matt. 6:19) is expounded in the next verse: "But lay up for yourselves treasures in heaven." "Labor not for the meat which perisheth" (John 6:27) is not an absolute prohibition, as the "but for that meat which endureth unto everlasting life" shows. Likewise, "Look not every man on his own things, but every man also on the things of others" (Phil. 2:4): we must love our neighbors as ourselves. "So then neither is he that planteth any thing, neither he that watereth" is to be taken relatively, for God frequently employs both the one and the other as instruments to do those very things: "but *God* that giveth the increase" (I Cor. 3:7) shows where the emphasis is to be placed, and the One to whom the glory is to be ascribed. "Whose adorning let it not be that outward adorning of plaiting the hair, and of wearing of gold, or of putting on of apparel; But let it be the hidden man of the heart, in that which is not corruptible . . . a meek and quiet spirit, which is in the sight of God of great price" (I Peter 3:3, 4).

There are, however, numerous examples that are not immediately explained for us, but which the Analogy of Faith makes clear. "And God spake unto Moses, and said unto him, I am the Lord: And I appeared unto Abraham, unto Isaac, and unto Jacob, by the name of God Almighty; but by My name *Jehovah* was I *not known* to them" (Exod. 6:2, 3). Yet it is quite plain from the words of Abraham in Genesis 15:6, 8, from his calling the altar "Jehovah-jireh" (Gen. 22:14), from Genesis 26:2, 24, and from God's words to Jacob in 28:13, that the patriarchs *were* acquainted with this Divine title. But they did not know Him as the Fulfiller of His promises or in His actual covenant faithfulness; whereas Moses and the Hebrews were now to be given proof of His word in Genesis 15:13, 14, and be brought into the land of Canaan. "Mine eyes are *ever* toward the Lord" (Ps. 25:15) must be understood in harmony with other Scriptures which show there were times when David's eyes were turned away from the Lord, and, as the result, he fell into grievous sins; nevertheless that was *the habit* of his heart, the general tenor of his spiritual life. See I Kings 15:5, for another comparative statement about David.

"Sacrifice and offering Thou didst not desire" any longer continued, as what follows shows — the shadows giving place to the substance: "burnt offering and sin offering hast Thou not required" (Ps. 40:6). Those last words are obviously to be understood relatively, for such offerings *were* then required by Divine appointment. But the presentation of the most costly sacrifices (the ram, or a bullock) were unacceptable to Him unless they proceeded from those who sincerely desired to obey and serve Him, as is clear from such passages as Proverbs 21:27; Isaiah 1:11-15. Comparative conformity to the precepts of the *moral* Law was of much greater importance than compliance with the ceremonial (see I Sam. 15:22; Ps. 69:30, 31; Prov. 21:3; Hos. 6:6; I Cor. 7:19). Worship is rejected unless proffered by love and gratitude. Similarly are we to understand, "For I spake not unto your fathers, nor commanded them in the day that I brought them out of Egypt, concerning burnt offerings or sacrifices" (Jer. 7:22) — those were not the primary or principal things I enjoined. No, "But *this* thing commanded I them, saying, Obey My voice": the design of the whole revelation at Sinai being to inculcate practical subjection to God's will, the Levitical ritual being a means to that end.

Words that are used to express *perpetuity* are not to be stretched any farther than the known duration of the things spoken of. As when the Jews were commanded to keep certain institutions throughout their generations to be ordinances for ever (Exod. 12:24; Num. 15:15), it was not signified they were to do so throughout eternity, but only during the Mosaic economy. Likewise the everlasting mountains and perpetual hills of Habakkuk 3:6, spoke only of *comparative* permanency and stability, for the earth is yet to be destroyed. "But when thou doest alms, let not thy left hand know what thy right hand doeth" (Matt. 6:3). Neither is this to be taken absolutely, otherwise any act of beneficence which came under the cognizance of our fellows would be prohibited, and that would be contrary to the Analogy of Faith. The primitive Christians did not always conceal their donations, as Acts 11:29, 30, demonstrates.

Secrecy itself may become a cloak of avarice, and under the pretence of hiding good works we may hoard up money to spend upon ourselves. There are times when a person of prominence may rightly excite his backward brethren by his own spirit of liberality. This Divine precept was designed to restrain the corrupt ambition of our hearts after the praise of men. Christ meant that we are to perform deeds of charity as unobtrusively as possible, making it our chief concern to have the approbation of God rather than the applause of our fellows. When a good work has been done, we should dismiss it from our minds, and instead of congratulating ourselves upon it, press on to other duties which are yet before us.

We are not to conclude from the terms of Luke 14:12, 13, that it is wrong for us to invite our friends and relatives to partake of our hospitality, though a comparative is there again expressed in positive language; but rather must we see to it that the poor and needy are not neglected or slighted by us. "For the law was given by Moses, but grace and truth came by Jesus Christ" (John 1:17). How often have those words been misunderstood, yea, wrested; for it is a serious mistake to conclude from them either that there was *no* "grace" under the Mosaic economy or that there is no "law" under the Christian. The fact is that the contrast is not between the messages of Moses and Christ, but the characteristics of their ministries. "Ye see Me *no more*" (John 16:10), said Christ to His apostles. Yet they *did!* What then did He mean? That they should not see Him again in a state of humiliation, in the form of a Servant, in the likeness of sin's flesh — compare *"like unto* the Son of man" (Rev. 1:13) because then in His *glorified* state. Acts 1:3, definitely informs us that Christ was seen of the apostles for forty days after His resurrection, and, of course, He is now seen by them in heaven. When the apostle declared, "I determined not to know any thing among you, save Jesus Christ, and Him crucified" (I Cor. 2:2), he did not mean that that was his sole theme, but rather that such was his dominant and prominent subject. When we are exhorted "be careful *for nothing*" (Phil. 4:6), we certainly are not to understand that care to please God is excluded, or that we are not to have deep concern for our sins.

The above examples (many others could be added) show that constant care is needed to distinguish between positive and comparative statements, and between words with an absolute force and those with merely a relative one.

11

15. *Non-literal language.* We have left this important canon of exegesis until a somewhat late stage, because maturity of judgment is called for in the applying of the same. There is a considerable amount of non-literal language in the Word of God and it is very necessary that the expositor should recognize the same. Great harm has been done through failure to do so, and not a few serious errors have been taught as the result of regarding what was figurative as literal. Generally speaking, the words of Scripture are to be understood in their plain and simple meaning; yea, their natural and obvious signification is always to be retained unless some evident and necessary reason requires otherwise; as, for example, when Christ bids us pluck out a right eye and cut off a right hand if the same causes us to sin, or when He charged the scribes and Pharisees with "devouring widows' houses" (Matt. 23:14), for manifestly such language is not to be taken at its face value. But there are many other instances which are not nearly so apparent as those, as when Christ said "*by chance* there came down a certain priest that way" (Luke 10:31), meaning that he took that direction without any particular purpose or special design — for a literal understanding of those words would deny the orderings of Providence.

Keen discrimination, both spiritual and mental, is required for distinguishing between the literal and the non-literal in Scripture. That applies in the first place to *the translator,* as a few simple illustrations will show. He has to determine in each occurrence of the word *kelayoth* whether to render it literally "kidneys" or figuratively "reins": our Authorized Version gives the former eighteen times, and the later thirteen. In such passages as Psalms 16:7; 26:2; 73:21, "reins" has reference to the *inner man,* particularly the mind and conscience: as the kidneys are for eliminating the impurities of the blood, so the mind and conscience are to deliver us from evil. The Hebrew word *ruach* literally means wind, and is so rendered ninety times in the Authorized Version; yet it is also used emblematically of *the spirit,* often of the Holy Spirit, and is so over 200 times. Much spiritual wisdom and discernment is required by the translator to discriminate. *Lachash* is rendered "earrings" in Isaiah 3:20, but "prayer" in Isaiah 26:16! The Greek word *presbuteros* literally means an aged person, and is so rendered in Acts 2:17, and Philemon 9, but in most cases it refers to "elders" or church officers.

Now if great care needs to be taken by the translator in distinguishing between things that differ, equally so of the expositor. Let him duly lay to heart the warnings supplied by the experience of the apostles. How often they failed to grasp the meaning of their Master's language! When He declared, "Not that which goeth into the mouth defileth a man; but that which cometh out of the mouth," they said unto Him, "Declare unto us this *parable,*" and He answered, "Are ye also yet without understanding?" (Matt. 15:11, 15, 16). When He bade them "beware of the leaven of the Pharisees and of the Sadducees" they reasoned among themselves and concluded that it was because they had taken no bread (Matt. 16:6, 7). When He told them that He had meat to eat that they knew not of, they imagined that someone had ministered to His bodily needs during their absence (John 4:32, 33). When He said, "Our friend Lazarus sleepeth," they supposed (as any of us would have done!) that He referred to natural sleep. How often is it recorded that they "understood not" the words of Christ (Mark 9:32; Luke 18:34; John 8:27; 12: 16). They quite missed His meaning when He asked, "If I will that he tarry till I come, what is that to thee?" (John 21:22, 23).

The figurative element is very prominent in the Scriptures, especially so in the Old Testament, where natural things are commonly used and accommodated to explain spiritual things, suiting its instructions to man's present state, in which he cannot see the things of God except through the glass of nature. Every Hebrew word has a literal sense and stands for some sensible object, and therefore conveys a comparative idea of some impalpable object. While in the body we must receive information via our senses. We cannot of ourselves form the least idea of any Divine or celestial object but as it is compared to and illustrated by something earthly or material. Inward realities are explained by outward phenomena, as in "rend your heart, and not your garments, and turn unto the Lord your God" (Joel 2:13), and "blessed are they which do hunger and thirst after righteousness." Spiritual mercies are set before our eyes under their familiar but expressive pictures in nature, as in "For I will pour water upon him that is thirsty, and floods upon the dry ground: I will pour *My Spirit* upon thy seed, and My blessing upon thine offspring" (Isa. 44:3), and "Drop down, ye heavens, from above, and let them bring forth salvation" (Isa. 45:8).

Others before us have pointed out that there is a Divinely designed analogy between the natural and the spiritual worlds. God so framed the visible realms as to shadow forth the invisible, the temporal to symbolize the eternal. Hence the similitudes so often employed by Christ, drawn by Him from the natural kingdom, were not arbitrary illustrations, but pre-ordained figures of the supernatural. There is a most intimate connection between the spheres of creation and of grace, so that we are taught thereby to look from one to the other. "By means of His inimitable parables, Christ showed that when nature was consulted aright it spoke one language with the Spirit of God; and that the more thoroughly it is understood, the more complete and varied will be found the harmony which subsists between the principles of its constitution and those of His spiritual kingdom" (P. Fairbairn). Who can fail to perceive both the aptness and the sublimity of the parallel between that allusion from the natural realm and its antitypical realization: "Until the day break, and the shadows flee away" (Song of Sol. 2:17), where the reference is to both the first (John 8:56) and second appearing of God's Son in the flesh (Phil. 1:6, 10)?

Words are used in a literal sense when given their plain and natural meaning; figuratively, when a term is diverted to an object to which it does not naturally or normally belong. Thus "hard" is the quality of a stone, but when predicated of the heart it is employed figuratively. A figure of speech consists in the fact of a word or words being used out of their ordinary sense and manner, for the sake of emphasis, by attracting our attention to what is said. Not that a different meaning is given to the word, but a new application of it is made. The meaning of the word is always *the same* when rightly used, and thus figures carry their own light and explain themselves. In the great majority of instances there is no difficulty in distinguishing between the literal and the non-literal. Here too there is a close resemblance between the Word of God and His works in creation. For the most part objects in the natural world are plain and simple, easily distinguished; yet some are obscure and mysterious. There are certain "laws" perceptible which regulate the actions of nature; nevertheless, there are notable exceptions to most of them. Thus we may be sure that God has not employed language which could only confuse and confound the unlearned, yet the meaning of many things in His Word can be ascertained only by hard labor.

If all Scripture had been couched in highly figurative language and mysterious hieroglyphics, it had been quite unsuited to the common man. On the other hand, if all were as simple as the A B C there had been no need for God to provide teachers (Eph. 4:11). But how is the teacher to determine when the language is literal and when non-literal? Generally, plain intimation is given, especially in the employment of metaphor, where one object is used to set forth another, as in "Judah is a lion's whelp" (Gen. 49:9). More particularly. First, when a literal interpretation would manifestly clash with the essential nature of the subject spoken of, as when physical members are ascribed to God, or when the disciple is required to "take up his cross" (live a life of self-sacrifice) in order to follow Christ. Second, when a literal interpretation would involve an absurdity or a moral impropriety, as in "When thou sittest to eat with a ruler, consider diligently what is before thee: and put a knife to thy throat, if thou be a man given to appetite" (Prov. 23:1, 2): giving no quarter to your lusts; and heaping coals of fire on an enemy's head (Rom. 12:20). Third, refer to other passages, and interpret such a verse as Psalm 26:6, by Genesis 35:1, 2, and Hebrews 10:22.

From all that has been said above it is evident that we must avoid a stark literalism when dealing with sensory or material representations of immaterial things, and when bodily terms are used of non-bodily ones. "The sword shall devour" (Jer. 46:10): to devour is the property of a living creature with teeth, but here by a figure it is applied to the sword. "Let my right hand forget her cunning" (Ps. 137:5): here "forgetting," which pertains to the mind, is applied to the hand — signifying "may it lose its power to direct aright." "I turned to see the voice" (Rev. 1:12) means Him that uttered it. "Keep thy foot when thou goest to the house of God" (Eccles. 5:1) may be taken in both a literal and a figurative sense. In the former, it would signify "let your gait be demure and your speed unhurried and reverent as you approach the place of worship"; in the latter, "pay attention to the motions of your mind and the affections of your heart, for *they* are to the soul what the feet are to the body." It is unto the due ordering of our inward man that our attention should be chiefly directed.

It is also very necessary for the expositor constantly to bear in mind that many of the things pertaining to the new covenant are set forth under the figures of the old. Thus Christ is spoken of as "our Passover" and as Priest "after the order of Melchisedec" (Heb. 6:20). Paradise is described as "Abraham's bosom" (Luke 16:22). The New Testament saints are referred to as Abraham's seed and "the Israel of God" (Gal. 3:7; 6:16); as "the circumcision" (Phil. 3:3), and as "a chosen generation, a royal priesthood, an holy nation" (I Peter 2:9); while in Galatians 4:26, they are informed that "Jerusalem which is above is free, which is the mother of us all." Again, the "For ye are not come unto the mount that might be touched" (Heb. 12:18) refers not to any material mount, but to that order of things which was formally instituted at Sinai, the moral features of which were suitably symbolized and strikingly adumbrated by the physical phenomena which attended the giving of the Law. Likewise, "ye are come unto mount Sion" (12:22) no more signifies a material mount than "we have an altar" (13:10) means that Christians have a tangible altar. It is the antitypical, spiritual, heavenly Sion which is in view — that glorious state into which Divine grace has brought all who savingly believe the Gospel.

Again, the expositor needs to be on the alert to detect *ironical language*, for it usually signifies the very opposite to what is expressed, being a form of satire for the purpose of exposing an absurdity and to hold up to ridicule. Such language was employed by God when He said, "Behold, the man is become as one of Us, to know good and evil" (Gen. 3:22), and when He bade Israel, "Go and cry unto the gods which ye have chosen; let them deliver you in the time of your tribulation" (Judg. 10:14); by Elijah, when he mocked the prophets of Baal: "Cry aloud: for he is a god; either he is . . . in a journey, or peradventure he sleepeth, and must be awakened" (I Kings 18:27); by Micaiah when he answered Jehoshaphat, "Go, and prosper: for the Lord shall deliver it into the hand of the king" (I Kings 22:15); by Job, "No doubt but ye are the people, and wisdom shall die with you" (12:2); in Ecclesiastes 11:9: "Rejoice, O young man, in thy youth . . . walk in the ways of thine heart, and in the sight of thine eyes"; by Christ, when He said, "A goodly price that I was prised at of them" (Zech. 11:13); and by Paul, "now ye are rich, ye have reigned as kings without us" (I Cor. 4:8).

Nor are we to take literally the *language of hyperbole* or exaggeration, when more is said than is actually meant, as when the ten spies said of Canaan, "the cities are great and walled up to heaven" (Deut. 1:28), and when we are told that their armies were "even as the sand that is upon the sea shore in multitude" (Josh. 11:4). So too the description given of those that came up against Gideon: "like grasshoppers for multitude; and their camels without number" (Judg. 7:12), and "there is no nation or kingdom, whither my lord hath not sent to seek thee" (I Kings 18:10). Further examples are found in: "They mount up to the heaven, they go down again to the depths" (Ps. 107:26); "Rivers of water run down mine eyes" (Ps. 119:136); "A little one shall become a thousand, and a small one a strong nation: I the Lord will hasten it in his time" (Isa. 60:22); "Their widows are increased to Me above the sand of the seas" (Jer. 15:8), which should be borne in mind when reading Revelation 7:9; "And there are also many other things which Jesus did, the which, if they should be written every one, I suppose that even the world itself could not contain the books that should be written" (John 21:25).

16. *The elucidation of the types.* No treatise on hermeneutics would be complete if it ignored this important and interesting department of exposition. Yet such a vast field pertains thereto that it is impossible to do it justice in a few sentences. The New Testament plainly teaches that there is not a little in the Old which anticipated and adumbrated things to come. From earliest times it pleased God to prepare the way for the grand word of redemption by a series of parabolical representations, and the business of the interpreter is to explain the same in the light of the fuller revelation which God has vouchsafed since then. Types belong to that sphere which concerns the relation of God's earlier and later dispensations, and therefore a type may be defined as a model or sign of another object or event which it depicted beforehand, shadowing forth something which should later correspond to and provide the reality of the same. But the question arises, How are we to avoid the erroneous and the extravagant in our selection and unfolding of the types? Space will only allow us to offer the following hints and rules.

First, there must be a genuine resemblance in form or spirit between any person, act or institution under the Old Testament and what answers to it in the Gospel. Second, a real type must be something which had its ordination from God, being meant by Him *to foreshadow* and prepare the way for the better things under Christ. Thus the resemblance between the shadow and the substance must be real and not fancied, and designed as such in the original institution of the former. It is that previous intention and pre-ordained connection between them which constitutes the relation of type and antitype. Third, in tracing out the connection between the one and the other, we have to inquire, What was the native import of the original symbol? What did it symbolize as a part of the then existing religion? And then the expositor is to proceed and show how it was fitted to serve as a guide and stepping-stone to the blessed events and issues of Messiah's kingdom. For example, by means of the tabernacle and its services God manifested toward His people precisely the same principles of government, and required from them substantially the identical disposition and character, that He does now under the higher dispensation of Christianity. Fourth, due regard must be had to the essential difference between the actual natures of the type and the antitype: the one being material, temporary and external; the other spiritual, eternal and often internal.

12

17. *Exposition of the parables.* This is another branch of our subject to which at least one whole chapter should be devoted, but the danger of overtaxing the patience of some of our readers renders it inadvisable. Because of the great simplicity of their nature and language, it is commonly supposed that the parables are more easily understood than any other form of scriptural instruction, when the fact is that probably more erroneous teaching has been given out through misapprehending the force of some of *their* details than is the case with anything else in the Word. Great care needs to be taken with them: especially is it important to ascertain and then keep in mind *the scope* or leading design of each one. But instead of so doing, only too often they are approached solely for the purpose of finding apparent support for some particular doctrine or idea which the preacher desires to prove. And in consequence, not a little in them has been wrested from its original purport, and made to signify what is flatly contradicted by other passages. Here, too, the Analogy of Faith must be held steadily in view, and our interpretation of each parable made to square therewith.

The children's definition that "a parable is an earthly story with a heavenly meaning" expresses the general idea. It is a form of teaching whereby spiritual things are represented under sensible images. Parables are virtually *word pictures,* bearing somewhat the same relation to the instruction of those to whom they are addressed as do the pictorial illustrations used in books to elucidate for the reader the printed page. From the relation to the truth presented or lesson enforced can be gathered certain important but simple and obvious principles, which need to be borne in mind in the study of our Lord's parables. First, the parable, as an illustrative picture, can only present its subject *partially.* No picture can give every aspect or exhibit every side of its object, any more than an architect's "ground plan" of a building shows its second and third stories, far less depict it as when completed — though it might *suggest* something of them. So a parable sketches for us only certain aspects of the subject. Hence we find them in groups: all in a group representing the same subject, but each one setting forth a distinct feature of the same — as in those of Matthew 13, dealing with the "mysteries of the kingdom of heaven." Hence, too, those of Luke 15 show us not only grace *receiving* sinners; but seeking, finding, clothing, feasting them.

Second, parables are *subordinate* to direct teaching; being designed not for proof, but for illustration of a doctrine or duty. It is alway to be deplored when professing Christians are guilty of setting one part of the Scriptures against another, but when a parable is used to nullify some plain doctrine or commandment of God, absurdity is added to irreverence. Hence to appeal to Matthew 18:23-25, in proof that the God of all grace may revoke His forgiveness, or to deny man's responsibility on the ground that "the lost piece of silver" of Luke 15 portrays the sinner by an inanimate object, is both foolish and profane. Third, it is equally apparent that we must seek to determine Christ's *principal aim* of the chief moral lesson which He intended to enforce in each one: yet that obvious duty is much neglected. Only too often parables are treated as though their design was left open to conjecture and their lessons to uncertain inference. Such an impious idea and loose way of handling them is clearly refuted by those which Christ Himself explained to His disciples. Thus we are not left entirely to our own resources, for those interpreted by the Lord are to be regarded as specimens — each setting forth some distinct truth, every detail possessing a significance.

Fourth, it is important to obtain a right understanding of the parabolical *representation* itself, since it supplies the basis of the spiritual instruction. Unless we understand the natural allusion, we cannot give a satisfactory exposition of the language in which it is set forth. Care has also to be taken that we do not extend the representation beyond the bounds in which it was intended to move. That representation becomes obvious when we concentrate upon the leading idea of the parable and allow its details to make that more distinct. A parable must not be broken into parts but looked at as a whole, though let it not be forgotten that every detail contributes to its central truth, there being no mere verbiage. Usually *the context* makes clear what is its purpose and purport. Thus the parable of the king taking account of his servants (Matt. 18:23) was in reply to Peter's inquiry in verse 21; that of the rich fool in Luke 12 was occasioned by a spirit of covetousness on the part of one who desired to obtain a part of his brother's inheritance. Those in Luke 15 grew out of what is related in its opening verses. Parables bear upon the more fundamental aspects of duty and deportment rather than on the minute details of either.

As intimated above, much erroneous teaching has resulted from failure to heed those simple rules. Thus, certain theologians who are basically unsound on the Atonement have argued from the parable of the prodigal son that, since no sacrifice was needed to reconcile him to the Father or provide access to the bosom of His love, God pardons absolutely, out of pure compassion. But that is a manifest wresting of the parable, for it is not as a Father but as the righteous Governor that God requires a satisfaction to His justice. Equally so is it a serious misrepresentation of the grace of the Gospel if we reason from the parable of the unmerciful servant (Matt. 18:23-35) that Divine grace is ever exercised unto men *except through* a propitiatory sacrifice, a reparation made to the broken Law, which God has accepted (Rom. 3:24). Those parables were never intended to teach the *ground* of Divine forgiveness: it is wrong to force any parable to display a whole system of theology. Some have even drawn from Christ's forbidding His disciples to pluck up the tares an argument against the local church's exercising such a strict discipline as would issue in the disfellowship of heretical or disorderly members —

refuted by His teaching in Revelation 2 and 3, where such laxity is severely rebuked.

Equally dangerous and disastrous is that interpretation which has made the parable of the laborers in the vineyard teach salvation by works. Since the parable affords a notable example of the importance of heeding the setting, we will offer a few remarks thereon. After the rich young ruler's refusal to leave all and follow Christ, and His seeking to impress upon His disciples the solemn warning of that sad spectacle, Peter said, "Behold, we have forsaken all, and followed Thee; what shall we have therefore?" (Matt. 19:22-27). The Lord returned a twofold answer: the first part, as the question was legitimate, declaring that both here and hereafter there should be abundant reward to those who followed Him (vv. 28, 29). In the second part our Lord searched Peter's heart, intimating that behind his inquiry was a wrong spirit — a carnal ambition which He had so often to rebuke in the apostles: shown in their disputes as to which of them should be greatest in the kingdom and which should have the chief seats therein. There was a mercenary spirit at work in them which considered *they* had claim to higher wages than others: since they were *the first* to leave all and follow Christ, thereby magnifying their own importance and laying Him under obligations. Hence the parable of Matthew 20:1-15, is preceded by the words. "But many that are first shall be last; and the last shall be first," and followed by similar words.

Since there be no room to doubt that the parable of the laborers in the vineyard was designed to illustrate the words in Matthew 19:30, and 20:16, it is clear that it was never intended to teach the way of salvation — to interpret it so is entirely to miss its scope. The Lord's object was manifestly to impress upon His disciples that, unless they mortified the same, the evils of the heart were of such a character as to rob the earliest and most prolonged external devotion of all value, and that the latest and briefest service unto Him would, by reason of the absence of self-assertion, be deemed worthy in His sight of receiving reward equal to the former. Moreover, He would have them know that He would do what He would with His own — they must not dictate the terms of service. It has been justly observed by Trench in his notes on this parable that an "agreement was made by the *first* hired laborers (20:2) before they entered upon their labor — exactly the agreement which Peter wished to make: "what shall we have?" — while those subsequently engaged went in a simpler spirit, trusting that whatever was right and equitable the householder would give them."

18. *Words with different meanings.* There are many terms in the Scriptures which are by no means employed uniformly. Some have diverse senses, others are given varied shades of one general sense. That does not mean they are used arbitrarily or capriciously, still less in order to confuse the minds of the simple. Sometimes it is because the original term is too full to be expressed by a single English equivalent. Sometimes it occurs with another form of emphasis. More often it is the various applications which are made of it to several objects. Thus it is an im-

portant part of the expositor's task to trace out those distinctions, and, instead of confounding the same, make clear each fresh sense, and thus "rightly divide the word of truth." Thus the Greek word *Paracletos* is rendered "Comforter" of the Spirit in John's Gospel, but "advocate" of Jesus Christ in his first Epistle (2:1). There appears to be little in common between those expressions, but when we discover that the Greek term means "one called to one's side (to help)," the difficulty is removed, and the blessed truth is revealed that the Christian has *two* Divine Helpers: a practical and a legal; one within his heart and one in heaven; one ministering to him, the other engaged for him.

The Greek word *diatheke* occurs thirty-three times; its common meaning — like the Hebrew *berith* — being "covenant." In the Authorized Version it is so rendered twenty times, and "testament" thirteen. Now a covenant is, strictly speaking, a contract between two parties, the one promising to do certain things upon the fulfilment of certain conditions by the other; whereas a testament or will is where one bequeaths certain things as gifts. There seems to be nothing in common between the two concepts, in fact that which is quite contrary. Nevertheless we believe our translators rightly rendered the term *both ways,* though not always happily so: most certainly it should be "covenant" in II Corinthians 3:6; Revelation 11:19. It is rightly rendered "covenant" in Hebrews 8: 6, and "testament" in 9:15, for a statement is there made to illustrate a certain correspondency between the preparatory and the ultimate in God's dispensations. A will does not become valid while the person making it is alive: it can only take effect after his decease. Hebrews 9:15-17, treats of a disposition showing the manner in which men obtain an inheritance through the riches of Divine grace. Thus, instead of using *syntheke,* which more exactly expressed a covenant, the Holy Spirit designedly employed *diatheke,* which was capable of a *double* application.

Let us now consider a few examples wherein the same English word is given a number of variants. As in the well-known words of our Lord, "Let the dead bury their dead" (Matt. 8:22), so the word "see" is used in two different senses in Hebrews 2:8, 9: "But now we see not yet all things put under Him. But we see Jesus . . . crowned with glory, and honor," where the first refers to open sight, the second to faith's perception. "Ransom" is by *power* as well as by price. Sometimes God defended or delivered His people by destroying His enemies: Proverbs 21:18; Isaiah 43:4; Pharaoh and his hosts at the Red Sea. Many have been much perplexed by the markedly different applications made of the word "burden" in Galatians 6:2, 5: "Bear ye one another's burdens, and so fulfil the law of Christ. . . . Every man shall bear his own burden." The former has in view the burdens of the Christian's infirmities, which should be sympathetically, prayerfully and practically shouldered by his brethren and sisters. The latter has reference to individual responsibility, his personal state and destiny, which he must himself discharge, that cannot be shifted upon others. The Greek word for the former is "weights," or loads — calling for a friendly hand. The latter signifies a "charge," or trust imposed.

The meaning of the term "flesh" appears to be so obvious that many would regard it as quite a waste of time to look up its various connections in Scripture. It is hastily assumed that the word is synonymous with the physical body, and so no careful investigation is made. Yet, in fact, "flesh" is used in Scripture to include far more than the physical side of our being. We read of "the will of the flesh" (John 1:13) and "the works of the flesh" (Gal 5:19), some of which are acts of the mind. We are forbidden to make provision for the flesh (Rom. 13:14), which certainly does not mean that we are to starve or neglect the body. When it is said "the Word was made flesh" (John 1:14) we are to understand that He took unto Himself an entire human nature, consisting of spirit (Luke 23:46), soul (John 12:27), and body. "In the days of His flesh" (Heb. 5:7) signifies the time of His humiliation, in contrast with His present exaltation and glory. Again, the average reader of the Bible imagines that "the world" is the equivalent of the whole human race, and consequently many of the passages in which it occurs are wrongly interpreted. Many too suppose that the term "immortality" calls for no critical examination, concluding that it refers to the indestructibility of the soul. But we must never assume that we understand anything in God's Word. If the concordance be consulted it will be found that "mortal" and "immortal" are never applied to man's soul, but always to his *body*.

"Holy" and "sanctify" represent in our English Bibles one and the same Hebrew and Greek word in the original, but they are by no means employed with a uniform significance, being given quite a variety of scope and application — hence the diverse definitions of men. The word is such a pregnant one that no single English term can express it. That it signifies more than "set apart" is clear from what is said of the Nazarite: "all the days of his separation he is *holy* unto the Lord (Num. 6:8) — "all the days of his separation he is separated" would be meaningless tautology. So of Christ, "holy, harmless, undefiled, separate from sinners" (Heb. 7:26), where "holy" means much more than "separate." When applied to God it imports His ineffable majesty (Isa. 57:15). In many passages it expresses a moral quality (Rom. 7:12; Titus 1:8). In others it refers to cleansing (Eph. 5:26; Heb. 9:13). Often it means to hallow or dedicate to God (Exod. 20:11; John 17:19). As the term is applied to the Christian it connotes, broadly speaking, (1) that sacred relationship Godward into which grace has brought us in Christ; (2) that blessed inward endowment by which the Spirit has made us meet for God and capacitated us to commune with Him; (3) the changed life resulting therefrom (Luke 1:75; I Peter 1:15).

The word "judgment" is another which calls for real study. There are judgments of God's *mouth* which His servants must faithfully declare (Ps. 119:13), namely the whole revelation of His will, the rule by which we are to walk and by which He will yet judge us. Those "judgments" (Exod. 21:1) are the Divine edicts which make known the difference between right and wrong. There are also judgments of God's *hand*: I know, O Lord, that Thy judgments are right, and that Thou in faithfulness hast afflicted me" (Ps. 119:75). Those are for the gracious discipline of His children; whereas those upon the wicked (Ezek. 5:15) are judicial curses and punishments. In some passages they express the whole of God's providential ways, many of which are "a great deep" (Ps. 36:6), "unsearchable" (Rom. 11:33) to any finite mind, not to be pried into by us. They intimate His sovereign rule, for "righteousness and judgment are the habitation of His throne" (Ps. 97:2), likewise the rectitude of Christ's administration (John 9:39). "He shall bring forth judgment to the Gentiles" (Isa. 42:1) imports the righteous doctrine of His Gospel. In Jude 14 and 15 the reference is to the solemn transactions of the last day. "Teach me good judgment and knowledge" (Ps. 119:66) is a request for discretion, a clearer apprehension to apply knowledge rightly. To "*do* justice and judgment" (Gen. 18:19) signifies to be equitable and just in our dealings.

13

19. *The Holy Spirit's use of words.* The correct interpretation of many passages can be satisfactorily established only by a careful investigation of how their terms are employed by the sacred writers, for not a few of them possess an entirely different force from their dictionary meanings. The signification of the words of Holy Writ is to be determined neither by their etymology nor by the sense which they bear in classical writings, but rather by their actual *use* in the Hebrew and Greek Scriptures — with the collateral help of the Septuagint version. Each term must be defined in strict harmony with the sense given to it in the Word itself. It is because the average reader of the Bible interprets much of its language in accord with how the same is employed in the common speech of his fellows that he has an inadequate, and often degrading, concept of its expressions. The concordance will stand him in far better stead than the best dictionary. Take the word "chasten." Upon human lips it means to punish, but such is far from the thought when we read of God's using the rod upon His children — even "for correction" falls far short. *Paideia* is only another form of *paidon,* which signifies "young children" (John 21: 5). One can see at a glance the direct connection which exists between "disciple" and "discipline": equally clear in the Greek is the relation between "chasten" and "child" — *son-training* expresses it more accurately (Heb. 12:7).

Consider the grand truth and glorious privilege of *adoption.* Probably it is not going too far to say that only a very small percentage of Christians entertain any scriptural concept thereof. In human affairs it has reference to a procedure whereby a boy or girl who bears no relation to a man and woman becomes legally their child. From that the conclusion is drawn that on the ground of Christ's atoning sacrifice and by the Spirit's work of regeneration those who previously bore no intimate relation to God then become His children. Such an idea is not only crude, but utterly erroneous. John 11:52, makes it quite clear that Christ died for His people under the consideration of their *being* the children of God, and not in order to make them so: as both the Hebrews in Egypt (Exod. 5) and the heathen in Corinth (Acts 18:10) were owned by God as His *before* the one was redeemed and the other had the Gospel preached unto them. "And because ye *are sons* [and not to make them such], God hath sent forth the Spirit of His Son into your hearts, crying, Abba, Father" (Gal. 4:6). The Spirit is given to quicken, communicate the nature of sons, and reveal to us our union with Christ.

The inestimable blessing of adoption was bestowed upon the elect by predestination, it being God's design therein to make them His sons by a mere act of His sovereign will: "Having foreordained us unto adoption as sons through Jesus Christ unto Himself, according to the good pleasure of His will" (Eph.1:5). Thus it is neither what Christ has done for them nor what the Spirit works in them which makes them the children of God. Adoption refers to that state of grace into which the elect are brought by virtue of their union with Christ. It is a *sonship-in-law*, in and through the Son, God appointing them unto union and communion with Him. Adoption conveys the legal right to every blessing we enjoy both here and hereafter. "The Spirit itself beareth witness with our spirit, that we are the children of God: and if children, then heirs of God, and joint-heirs with Christ" (Rom. 8:16, 17). As holiness is that which fits us for heaven, so adoption or sonship conveys *the right* thereto. "Adoption does not so much design the blessing itself prepared in the Divine predestination, or the grace received in effectual calling, as the inheritance to which the saints are adopted, even the heavenly glory: see Romans 8: 23" (J. Gill).

The elect were bestowed upon Christ before the foundation of the world in the relation of *children*: "Behold I and the children which God hath given Me" (Heb. 2:13) will be His own triumphant exclamation at the last day — not one of them lost. It is quite true that by the fall they became alienated from God, and thus in need of His being reconciled to them and they to Him; that they became dead in trespasses and sins, and therefore required to be quickened into newness of life. But observe closely how Galatians 4:4, 5 states it: "God sent forth His Son, made of a woman, made under the law, to redeem them [previously His] that were under the law, that we might *receive* the adoption of sons," and because we were such the Spirit was given to us. The declaration of adoption was made first in predestination (Eph. 1:5), afterwards in Christ, and then in the believer. As the Puritan Charnock so succinctly stated it, "Adoption gives us the *privilege* of sons, regeneration the *nature* of sons. Adoption *relates* unto God as a Father, regeneration *engraves* upon us the lineaments of a Father. That makes us *relatively* His sons by conferring a power or right (John 1:12); this makes us *formally* His sons by conveying a principle (I Peter 1:23). By that we are enstated in the Divine affection; by this we are partakers of the same."

"Think not that I am come to destroy the law, or the prophets: I am not come to destroy, but to fulfil" (Matt. 5:17). A momentous statement was that, and a right understanding thereof is essential, particularly of the exact meaning of its final word. Determined to deny at all costs the evangelical truth that Christ rendered to the Law a vicarious obedience on behalf of His people, Socinians insist that in this passage "fulfil" signifies to fill out or fill full. But such a definition is entirely arbitrary, and is refuted by the canon of interpretation we are now illustrating. As the scholarly Smeaton pointed out, "No example of such a usage can be adduced when the verb is applied to a law or to an express demand contained in the spirit of the law: in which case it uniformly means 'to fulfil'. Thus it is said, 'he that loveth another hath fulfilled [i.e., kept] the law' (Rom. 13:8). The inflexible usage of language rules the sense in such a phrase, to the effect that Christ must be understood to say that He came not to fill out or to supplement the law by additional elements, but to fulfil it by being made under it.

"Second, 'fill out' is inadmissible as applied to the second term or object of the verb: Christ did not come to fill out or expound the prophets, but simply to fulfil their predictions. Whenever the word here used is applied to anything prophetical, it is always found in such a connection that it can only mean 'to fulfil,' and hence we must not deviate from its uniform signification. Third, the eighteenth verse must be regarded as giving a reason for the statement made in the seventeenth. But what sort of a reason would be given if we were to render the connected verses thus: I am come to fill out or supplement the law, for verily I say unto you, Till heaven and earth pass, one jot or one tittle shall in no wise pass from the law, till all be fulfilled'?" Moreover, it is to be carefully noted that the term fulfil was here placed by Christ in direct antithesis to "destroy," which further determines its scope and meaning, for to destroy the law is not to empty it of its meaning, but to rescind or abrogate it. Thus to "fulfil" is to be taken in its plain and natural sense, as meaning to perform what the Law and the prophets required: to substantiate them, to make good what they demanded and announced. Law can only be fulfilled by a perfect obedience being rendered to it.

What has just been before us leads us to point out that the only sure and satisfactory way of settling the old controversy between the Protestant and popish theologians as to whether the word "justify" means to *make* just or to *pronounce* just is to ascertain *how* the term is used by the sacred writers, for an appeal to Holy Writ does not leave the issue in the slightest doubt. In the first place, when we are said to "glorify God" we do not render Him glorious, but announce that He is so. When we are bidden to sanctify the Lord God in our hearts (I Peter 3:15), we do not make Him holy, but assert that He is so. Equally, when it is said "that Thou mightest be justified when Thou speakest, and be clear when Thou judgest" (Ps. 51:4), the force of it is that Thou mightest be pronounced righteous in Thy judicial verdicts. In none of these instances is there the least ambiguity or uncertainty, in none is there any transformation wrought in the object of the verb — to suggest so would be horrible blasphemy. When wisdom is said to be "justified of her children" (Matt. 11:19) it obviously signifies that she is vindicated by them. Nor does the word have any different force when it is applied to the sinner's acceptance with God.

In the second place, it is to be noted that in many passages justification is placed over against *condemnation*. The meaning of a term is often perceived by weighing the one that is placed in opposition to it — as "destroy" is over against "fulfil" in Matthew 5:17. "If there be a controversy between men, and they come unto judgment, that the judges may judge them; then they shall justify the righteous, and condemn the wicked" (Deut. 25:1). "He that justifieth the wicked, and he that condemneth the just, even they both are abomination to the Lord" (Prov. 17:15). "For by thy words thou shalt be justified, and by thy words thou shalt be condemned" (Matt. 12:37). Thus the forensic sense of the term is definitely established, for in those and similar passages two judicial sentences are mentioned which are exactly the reverse of each other. As to condemn a man "is *not to make him* unrighteous, but is simply the pronouncing of an adverse sentence against him, so to justify is to not to effect any moral improvement in his character, but is simply declaring him *to be righteous.* The word is still further explained by Romans 3:19, 20: "that every mouth may be stopped, and all the world may become [be brought in] guilty before God: Therefore by the deeds of the law there shall no flesh be justified in His sight," where guilt and non-justification are synonymous.

But in all generations Satan and his agents have labored to make men believe that when Scripture speaks of God's justifying sinners it signifies the making of men righteous by means of something which is infused into them, or else produced by them; thereby dishonoring Christ. The early chapters of Romans are devoted to an exposition of this all-important truth. First, it is shown that "there is none righteous" (3:10), none who measures up to the Law's requirements. Second, that God has provided a perfect righteousness in and by Christ, and that this is revealed in the Gospel (1:16, 17; 3:21, 22). Third, that this righteousness, or vicarious obedience, of Christ is *imputed* or reckoned to the account of those who believe (4:11, 24). Fourth, that since God has placed to the credit of the believing sinner the fulfilment of the Law by his Substitute, he is justified (5:1, 18). Fifth, therefore none can lay anything to his charge (8:33). Thus may the believing sinner exultantly exclaim, "In the Lord have I righteousness and strength" (Isa. 45:24), "I will greatly rejoice in the Lord, my soul shall be joyful in my God; for He hath clothed me with the garments of salvation, He hath covered me with the robe of righteousness" (Isa. 61:10). "I will go in the strength of the Lord God: I will make mention of Thy righteousness, even of Thine only" (Ps. 71:16).

Many suppose when they read of the "foreknowledge" of God (Acts 2:23; I Peter 1:2) that the expression simply means His cognizing beforehand. It imports very much more, expressing infallible certainty because based upon His eternal decree. God foreknows what will be because He has purposed what shall be. In its verbal form the word is actually rendered "foreordained" rather than "foreknown" in I Peter 1:20. Some Arminians, in their inveterate opposition to the Truth, have insisted that the word "elect" means a choice or excellent person, rather than a selected one, appealing to Christ's being termed God's "elect" in Isaiah 42:1. But the Holy Spirit has anticipated and refuted that wretched shift by defining the term in Matthew 12:18 (where He cites Isa. 42:1), "Behold My servant, whom I have chosen." Mark 13:20, settles the meaning of "elect" once for all: "the elect's sake, *whom He hath chosen.*" In common speech "prince" signifies one who is inferior to the king, but not when Christ is called "the Prince of peace" and "the Prince of life," as is clear from His being "Prince of the kings of the earth" (Rev. 1:5). Many have been puzzled over mustard being called "the greatest among herbs" (Matt. 13:22), and love being greater than faith (I Cor. 13:13), when in fact faith is its root: but "greatest" does not mean largest in the former, or superior in the latter, but *the most useful* — the "best gifts" of I Corinthians 12:31, and "greater" in I Corinthians 14:5, signify more useful.

20. *Distinguish between things that differ,* for if we do not the Bible will at once appear to contradict itself, and our minds will be in a state of hopeless confusion. If we carelessly generalize and confound things apart, not only shall we form a vague conception of them, but in many instances a thoroughly erroneous one. Most necessary is it that the expositor attend diligently to this rule: only so will he be able to give the true explanation of many a verse. Not only is it important to discriminate between two diverse things, but often to draw distinctions between various aspects of the same subject. Take, first, the word "care." In Luke 10:41, we find our Lord rebuking Martha because she was "careful and troubled about many things," and His servant wrote, "I would have you *without carefulness*" (I Cor. 7:32); while in Philippians 4:6, Christians are exhorted to "be careful for nothing." On the other hand, we are exhorted that there should be no division in the local church, "but that the members should have the same care one for another" (I Cor. 12:25), and the apostle commended penitent saints for the "carefulness" it wrought in them and expressed his own concern for their welfare by referring to "our care" for them (II Cor. 7:11, 12). Thus there is a "care" which is forbidden and a care that is required. The one is a godly and moderate solicitude, which moves to watchfulness and the taking of pains in the performing of duty; the other is a distrustive and inordinate one that produces distraction and worry.

In like manner we must distinguish sharply between two totally different kinds of *fear*: the one which is becoming, spiritual, and helpful; the other carnal, worthless, hurtful. Believers are bidden to work out their own salvation with fear and trembling (Phil. 2:12), that is with a conscientious horror of displeasing the One who has been so gracious to them. Conversely, "perfect love casteth out fear" (John 4:18), namely that slavish dread which causes torment, those terrifying thoughts which make us look forward to the day of judgment with dismay. "God is greatly to be feared" (Ps. 89:7): that is, held in the highest esteem and reverence, the heart deeply impressed with His majesty, awed by His ineffable holiness. When we read of those who "feared the Lord, and served their own gods" (II Kings 17:33), it means that out of a dread of His vengeance they went through the outward form of worshipping Him, but that the love of their wicked hearts was set upon their idols. Thus a filial fear inspires with a grateful desire to please and honor God, but a servile fear produces terror in the mind because of a guilty conscience, as was the case with Adam (Gen. 3:9, 10), and is so now with the demons (James 2:19). The one draws to God, the other drives from Him; the one genders to bondage and leads to despair; the other works humility and promotes the spirit of adoration.

In order to understand certain passages it is absolutely needful to recognize that there is a *twofold* "will" of God spoken of in the Scriptures, by which we do not mean His decretive will and His permissive will, for in the final analysis that is a distinction without a difference, for God never permits anything which is contrary to His eternal purpose. No, we refer to the very real distinction which there is between His *secret* and His *revealed* will, or, as we much prefer to express it, between His predestinating and His preceptive will. God's secret will is His own counsels which He has divulged to no one. His revealed will is made known in His Word, and is the definer of our duty and the standard of our responsibility. The grand reason why I should follow a certain course or do a certain thing is because it is God's will that I should do so — made known to me in the rule I am to walk by. But suppose I go contrary to His Word and disobey, have I not crossed His will? Assuredly. Then does that mean that I have thwarted His purpose? Certainly not, for that is always accomplished, notwithstanding the perversity of His creatures. God's revealed will is never performed perfectly by any of us, but His secret or foreordinating will is never prevented by any (Ps. 135:6; Prov. 21:30; Isa. 46:10).

What has just been referred to above is admittedly a great deep, which no finite mind can fully fathom. Nevertheless, the distinction drawn *must* be made if we are not to be guilty of making the Scriptures contradict themselves. For example, such passages as the following evince the universality and invincibility of God's will being accomplished. "But He is in one mind, and who can turn Him? and what His soul desireth, even that He doeth" (Job 23:13). "But our God is in the heavens. He hath done whatsoever He hath pleased" (Ps. 115:3). "He doeth according to His will in the army of heaven, and among the inhabitants of the earth: and none can stay His hand, or say unto Him, "What doest Thou?" (Dan. 4:35). "For *who* hath resisted *His* will?" (Rom. 9:19). On the other hand, such passages as the following have reference to the revealed or *preceptive* will of God which may be withstood by the creature. "And that servant, which knew his Lord's will, and prepared not himself, neither did according to His will" (Luke 12:47). "For this is the will of God, even your sanctification" (I Thess. 4:3). "In every thing give thanks: for this is the will of God in Christ Jesus concerning you" (I Thess. 5:18). God's secret will is His eternal and unchanging purpose concerning all things which He has made, and is brought about by means and through agencies which He has appointed to that end, and which can no more be hindered by men or devils than they can prevent the sun from shining.

14

I~N~ view of certain passages in the Old Testament, not a few have been perplexed by that word, "No man hath seen God at any time" (John 1:18) — words once used as a stock argument by infidels to "prove that the Bible is full of contradictions." Such verses call for the interpreter: to explain their sense, and thereby distinguish between things that differ. Some of those statements which speak of the Lord's "appearing" to one and another of the ancient celebrities refer to His doing so as the Angel of the covenant; others were theophanic manifestations, wherein He assumed the human form (cf. Ezek. 1:26; Dan. 3:25), presaging the Divine incarnation; others mean that He was seen by faith (Heb. 11:26). When Isaiah declared, "I saw also the Lord sitting upon a throne, high and lifted up, and His train filled the temple" (6:1), it signifies that he did so with the eyes of his understanding, in prophetic vision, and not with his bodily sight. God, essentially considered, is "invisible" (I Tim. 1:17), for His essence or nature cannot be seen (I Tim. 6:16), no, not by the holy angels nor by the glorified saints in heaven. When it is said we shall see "face to face" (I Cor. 13:12), it imports "plainly and distinctly," in contrast with "through a glass, darkly" (obscurely) in the former part of the verse; though the Lord Jesus actually will be seen face to face.

A careful examination of the different passages in which our Lord is referred to as "coming" reveals the fact that by no means all of them allude to His personal and public return, when He shall "appear the second time without sin unto salvation" (Heb. 9:28). Thus, "I will not leave you comfortless: I will come to you" (John 14:18), which had reference, first, to His corporeate coming unto His disciples after His resurrection and, second, to His coming spiritually at Pentecost, when He gave them another Comforter. "If a man love Me, he will keep My words: and My Father will love him, and We will come unto him" (John 14:23) — come in the powerful influences of Divine grace and consolation. "And that He might reconcile both unto God in one body by the cross, having slain the enmity thereby: and *came* and preached peace to you which were afar off, and to them that were nigh" (Eph. 2:16, 17), which was accomplished mediately, in the ministry of His servants, for he who receives them receives Him (Matt. 10:40). "Remember therefore from whence thou art fallen, and repent, and do the first works; or else I will come unto thee quickly, and will remove thy candlestick out of his place" (Rev. 2:5, and cf. 2:16) — that is a judicial visitation. "He shall come unto us as the rain" (Hos. 6:3): every spiritual revival and bestowment of grace is a coming of the Lord unto the soul.

Another example where it is necessary to distinguish between things that differ is to observe carefully the various shades of meaning given to the word *hope*. In some passages the reference is to *the grace* of hope, the faculty by which we expect some future good, as in "faith, hope, charity" (I Cor. 13:13), of which God is the Author — "the God of hope" (Rom. 15:13). In some verses it is the *ground* of expectation, that on which it rests, as it is said of Abraham, "Who against hope believed in hope, that he might become the father of many nations," which is explained in what follows: "according to that which was spoken, So shall thy seed be" (Rom. 4:18) — his hope reposing upon the sure promise of God. In other places it is the *object* of hope that is in view, the things expected, or the One in whom our confidence is placed, as in "the hope which is laid up for you in heaven" (Col. 1:5), "looking for that blessed hope" (Titus 2:13), "O Lord, the hope of Israel" (Jer. 17:13). Occasionally the term signifies the *assurance* which is produced, as in "my flesh also shall rest in hope" (Ps. 16:9) and "rejoice in hope . . . hope maketh not ashamed" (Rom. 5:2, 5). *Four*

For clearness of thought and soundness of doctrine, it is most necessary to distinguish between the *three tenses* and the various aspects of God's *salvation*. Familiar as we are with that word, it is used with unpardonable looseness (even by the majority of preachers), through failure to recognize that it is the most comprehensive term to be found in the Scriptures, and to take the trouble of ascertaining how it is used therein. Only too often a most inadequate concept is formed of the scope and contents of that word, and through ignoring the distinctions which the Holy Spirit has drawn nothing but a blurred and jumbled idea is obtained. How few, for example, would be able to give a simple exposition of the following statements: "Who hath saved us" (II Tim. 1:9, and cf. Titus 3:5); "work out your own salvation with fear and trembling" (Phil. 2:12); "Now is our salvation nearer than when we believed" (Rom. 13:11, and cf. I Peter 1:5). Now these verses do not refer to three different salvations, but rather to three *aspects of* one salvation. The first as an accomplished fact — from the pleasure and penalty of sin. The second as a present process — from the power and ragings of sin. The third as a future prospect — from the very presence of sin.

If the balance of truth is to be preserved and the evil practice of pitting one aspect against another, or of over-emphasizing one and ignoring another, is to be avoided, a careful study needs to be made of the different *causes and means* of salvation. There are no less than seven things which concur in this great work, for all of them are said, in one passage or another, to "save" us. Salvation is ascribed to the Father: "Who hath saved us, and called us with an holy calling" (II Tim. 1:9) — because of His electing love in Christ. To the Lord Jesus: "He shall save His people from their sins" (Matt. 1:21) — because of His merits and satisfaction. To the Holy Spirit: "He saved us, by the . . . renewing of the Holy Ghost" (Titus 3:5) — because of His almighty and efficacious operations. To the instrumentality of the Word: "The engrafted word, which is able to save your souls" (James 1:21) — because it discovers to us our need and reveals the grace whereby we may be saved. To the labors of the Lord's servants: "in doing this thou shalt both save thyself, and them that hear thee (I Tim. 4:16) — because of their fidelity to the Truth. To the conversion of the sinner, in which both repentance and faith are exercised by him: "save yourselves from this untoward generation" (Acts 2:40) — by the repentance spoken of in verse 38: "by grace are ye saved through faith" (Eph. 2:8). To the ordinances: "baptism doth also now save us" (I Peter 3:21) — sealing the grace of God to a believing heart.

Now those seven concurring causes of salvation need to be considered in their order and kept in their proper places, otherwise incalculable harm will be done. For instance, if we elevate a subordinate cause above a primary one, then all sense of real proportion is lost. The love and wisdom of God are the root cause, the first mover of all else. Next are the merits and satisfaction of Christ, which are also the foundation of all else that follows. The effectual operations of the Holy Spirit produce in sinners those things which are necessary for their participation in the benefits purposed by the Father and purchased by Christ. The Word is the chief means employed by God in conviction and conversion. As the result of the Spirit's operation and the application of the Word in power to our hearts, we are brought to repent and believe. In this, it is the Spirit's usual custom to employ the minister of Christ as His subordinate agents. Baptism and the Lord's supper are means whereby we express our repentance and faith, and have them confirmed to us. Nor must those concurring causes be confounded, so that we attribute to a later one what pertains to an earlier one. We must not ascribe to the ordinances that which belongs to the Word, nor to conversion what originates through the Spirit, nor give to Him the honor which is peculiar to Christ. Each is to be carefully distinguished, defined, and kept in its proper place.

The need of distinguishing between things that differ is further evidenced by the following. The walking in darkness of Isaiah 1:10, is not occasioned by the Lord's withdrawing the light of His countenance, but is due to the absence of *ministerial instruction,* and therefore is to be explained by Amos 8:11; whereas the walking in darkness of I John 1:6, consists of an open revolt from God. The word "dead" in John 6:49, signifies physically; "not die" in the next verse means spiritually; "shall never see death" in John 8:51, has reference to the second death. The passing "from death unto life" of John 5:24, is legal, the reward of the Law — justification; but the passing "from death unto life" of I John 3:14, is experiential — regeneration. The "one new man" of Ephesians 2:15, is that mystical body which is composed of saved Jews and Gentiles, whereof Christ is the Head; whereas "the new man" of Ephesians 4:24, is the new state and standing secured by regeneration, and which the recipient is required to make manifest in his daily deportment. Christ's being "without sin" at His first advent (Heb. 4:15) means that He was personally and experientially so, being the Holy One of God; but His being "without sin" at His second advent (Heb. 9:28) imports imputatively so, no longer charged with the guilt of His people. In such passages as Romans 5:1; Ephesians 2:8; etc., "faith" signifies the act and grace of faith, but in I Timothy 3:9; 4:1; Jude 3, "the faith" refers to the body of doctrine revealed in Scripture.

21. *The spiritual meaning* of Scripture: not simply in the application which may fairly be made of a passage, but its actual content. We have in mind those passages where a material object or historical transaction adumbrated or contemplated spiritual objects and experiences. Great care needs to be exercised here, lest on the one hand we be such slaves to "literalism" that we miss the deeper significance and higher import of many things in God's Word; or lest on the other hand we give free rein to our imagination and "read into" a verse what is not there or "carnalize" what should be taken in its plain and natural sense. Against both of those evils the expositor needs to be constantly on his guard. Let it also be pointed out that in not a few instances the Scriptures possess both a literal and a mystical force, and one of the tasks devolving upon the interpreter is to bring out each of them clearly. A few examples will make our meaning simpler.

The first six verses of Psalm 19 contain a sublime description of the perfections of God as they are displayed in the material creation, especially in the heavenly bodies; yet it is quite evident that the apostle Paul also regarded what is there said of the sun and stars as their being Divinely designed emblems of the kingdom of grace. For in Romans 10: 4-17, we find that he had before him the universal publication of the Gospel, and that in verse 18 he quoted from Psalm 19: "But I say, Have they not heard? Yes, verily, their sound went into all the earth, and their words unto the ends of the world." Ministers of Christ are designated "stars" (Dan. 12:3; Rev. 1:20), for as the stars illumine all parts of the earth, so evangelical messengers scatter the rays of light and truth upon the darkness of an ungodly world. And as there is no speech or language where the voice of the celestial stars is not heard, for they are so many tongues proclaiming the glory of their Maker, so the ministers of Christ have, at different periods of history, heralded God's good news in every human tongue. On the day of Pentecost men of many nations heard God's servants speak in their own tongues the wonderful works of God, so that even then the line of the apostles' testimony "went through all the earth" (Acts 2:9-11, and cf. Col. 1:5, 6, 23).

The propriety of the apostle's spiritual interpretation of Psalm 19:4, is at once apparent, and it supplies us with an invaluable key for the opening of what immediately follows. In the light of Messianic predictions it is quite clear that what is said in verses 5 and 6 is to be understood, ultimately, of Christ Himself, for in Malachi 4:2, He is expressly called "the Sun of righteousness," who should "arise with healing in His wings." As the sun is a celestial body, so the Saviour is not a product of the earth (John 8:23), but is "the Lord from heaven" (I Cor. 15:47). Thus the Psalmist went on to say, "In them [the heavens] hath He set a tabernacle for the sun." Attention is focused upon the central luminary in the firmament, all the lesser ones being as it were lost sight of. So it is in the Gospel: one central Object alone is set forth and magnified therein. As the heavens, particularly the sun, exhibit the natural glory of

God, so the Gospel, in its revelation of the Son, makes manifest the moral glory of God. Most appropriately is the Gospel likened to a "tabernacle" or tent (rather than a fixed temple), for as Israel's of old, so it both contains and yet veils Christ's glory, and is designed to move freely from place to place, rather than be stationary.

"Which is as a bridegroom coming out of his chamber." Just as the sun in the early morning throws back the curtains of his pavilion, issuing forth to disperse the sombreness of night, so in the Gospel Christ appears as a Bridegroom, removing the darkness of unregeneracy from His people, to be loved and admired by all who believe. "And rejoiceth as a strong man to run a race," fully assured of His triumph (Rev. 6:2). "His going forth is from the end of the heaven, and his circuit unto the ends of it." In Micah 5:2, we are told that Christ's "*going forth* have been from of old, from the days of eternity" (margin). Those goings forth were, first, in that everlasting covenant which is ordered in all things and sure, wherein He promised "Lo, I come to do Thy will, O God." Second, in the announcements of prophecy, when, from Genesis 3:15, onwards, the curtains were thrown back wider and wider, for the person of the Messiah to appear in increasing distinctness, until in Isaiah 53 He stood forth fully revealed. Third, in the travels of the Gospel from one side of the earth to the other, which will continue until His yet grander appearing. When He shines into a soul "there is nothing hid from the heat thereof." This interpretation is confirmed by verse 7: "The law of the Lord is perfect, *converting* the soul."

The eighth Psalm supplies us with another example of a passage of Scripture having a *double* purport — a natural and also a spiritual. The principal scope of that psalm, as its opening and closing verses show, is to magnify the Creator — by extolling the wondrous works of His hands. As David beheld the beauties and marvels of the heavens, he had such a sense of his own nothingness that he exclaimed, "What is man [*enosh* — frail, puny man], that Thou art mindful of him? and the son of man [a diminution of "man"], that Thou visitest him?" Then his wonderment deepened as he went on to say, "For Thou hast made him a little lower than the angels, and hast crowned him with glory and honor. Thou madest him to have dominion over the works of Thy hands; Thou hast put all things under his feet." Therein we behold both the sovereignty and the abounding grace of God, in so highly elevating one so lowly. This filled the Psalmist with amazement and awe, that God should have placed all mundane creatures in subjection unto man rather than unto angels (Gen. 1:28). Therein we behold the goodness of God to mankind, and the high favor conferred upon them. But that by no means exhausts the scope and sense of those verses.

Psalm 8:4-6, is quoted by the apostle in Hebrews 2:6-8, where he was proving from Scripture the immeasurable superiority of Christ over angels. He was indeed for a little while (during the season of His humiliation) made lower than they, but after He had triumphantly concluded the work given Him to do, God exalted Him far above them. Thus, what was spoken indefinitely of "man" by David, Paul makes a definite and spiritual application of unto Christ, for after saying "we see not yet all things put under Him," he at once added "but we see Jesus," which signifies that we see accomplished in Him the terms of that ancient oracle. All room for doubt on that score is removed by Paul's next words, "who was made a little lower than the angels for the suffering of death, crowned with glory and honor." That Psalm 8 *is* a Messianic one is further seen by the passages cited from it in Matthew 21:16; I Corinthians 15:27, which unquestionably applies to the Lord Jesus. The language used by David, then, was far more than a natural outburst of admiration of God's works in creation, namely a spiritual ecstasy as he was granted an insight into the mystery of grace, the kingdom of Christ, and the love of the Father unto the person of the Mediator.

But the ravishment of David's spirit was excited by something more than what has just been pointed out: the "man" whom he contemplated was the "new man," the "perfect man" of Ephesians 2:15, and 4:13 — that *spiritual* Man of which Christ is the Head. David's utterance had respect, ultimately, not only unto Christ personal, but unto Christ mystical, for the Redeemer shares with His redeemed the spoils of His victory and admits them to a participation in His reward. They are His "joint-heirs" (Rom. 8:17), and it is *their glorification* which Psalm 8:5, 6, had in final view. Even now the angels are in a position of subordination to them (Heb. 1:14) and in a coming day the redeemed shall be "crowned with glory and honor." "To him that overcometh will I grant to sit with Me on My throne" (Rev. 3:21, and cf. 21:7). The exaltation of Christ is the guarantee of the Christian's, for He entered heaven as the firstfruits — the earnest of the coming harvest. Oh, what a prospect is there here for faith to lay hold of and hope to enjoy now! If it were more real to us, if we were more engaged in looking away from the present to the future, we should be filled with wonderment and praise, and the petty trials and troubles of this life would affect us much less than they do.

Psalm 89 supplies us with a further illustration of the principle we are here treating, and a very striking and important one it is. Historically it looks back to what is recorded in II Samuel 7:4-17, namely, the covenant which the Lord made with David; yet none with anointed eyes can read that Psalm without quickly perceiving that a greater than the son of Jesse is there in view, namely his Saviour. In the light of Isaiah 42:1, "I have made a covenant with My Chosen, I have sworn unto David My Servant" (Ps. 89:3), it is quite clear that the *spiritual reference* is to that covenant of grace which God made with the Mediator before the foundation of the world; compare "Then thou spakest *in vision* to Thy Holy One" (v. 19). This is further confirmed in what immediately follows: "Thy seed will I establish forever, and build up thy throne to all generations" (v. 4), which is not true of the historical David. As Spurgeon remarked, "David must always have a seed, and truly this is fulfilled in Jesus beyond his hopes. What a seed David has in the multitude which have sprung from Him who was both his Son and his Lord! The Son of David is the great Progenitor, the last Adam, the everlasting Father; He sees His seed, and in them beholds of the travail of His soul.

David's dynasty never decays, but on the contrary, is evermore consolidated by the great Architect of heaven and earth. Jesus is a King as well as a Progenitor, and His throne is ever being built up." As we read through this Psalm, verse after verse obliges us to look beyond the literal *to the spiritual*, until the climax is reached in verse 27, where God says of the antitypical David, "I will make Him My Firstborn, higher than the kings of the earth."

15

I Corinthians 10:1-4, furnishes another illustration of what we are here treating; to wit, *the spiritual content* of many passages in God's Word. "Moreover, brethren, I would not that ye should be ignorant, how that all our fathers were under the cloud, and all passed through the sea; And were all baptized unto Moses in the cloud and in the sea; And did all eat the same spiritual meat; And did all drink the same spiritual drink: for they drank of that spiritual Rock that followed them: and that Rock was Christ." As a matter of fact, historically, Divinely recorded, they partook of material food and drank of water which flowed from a literal rock; yet three times over the apostle declared that the same were *spiritual*. In so doing Paul was not merely intimating that there was a close analogy between God's dealings with the Hebrews of old and with His saints today: rather was he insisting that the wilderness experiences of Israel after the flesh adumbrated the soul experiences of Israel after the spirit. It is not only that the Divine institutions under Judaism possessed a symbolical and typical significance, but that Christians enter into the spiritual substance of which they were but the shadows. Christ is our altar (Heb. 13:10), our passover (I Cor. 5:7), our high priest (Heb. 4:14). In Him we are spiritually circumcised (Col. 2:11).

"But ye are come unto mount Sion" (Heb. 12:22) is also to be understood spiritually, and not literally. That should be quite obvious, yet, because of the gross and carnal ideas of modern Dispensationalists, there is need for us to labor the point. That is one of the many passages where the blessings and privileges of the new covenant are expressed in language taken from the old, the antitype being presented under the phraseology of the type. Thus, when Christ announced the free intercourse which now exists between heaven and earth, and which His redemptive work was to produce, He described it in words taken from Jacob's vision: "Verily, verily, I say unto you, Hereafter ye shall see heaven open, and the angels of God ascending and descending upon the Son of man" (John 1:51). Very remarkable and full was that statement, containing much more within it than has been discerned by the majority of expositors. It not only declared that there was to be restored a blessed intercourse between the holy spirits of the upper world and the saints while here in the lower one, but it also revealed the foundation on which that intercourse rests, furnishing the key to such passages as Acts 12:7, and Hebrews 1:14. It is to be carefully noted that Christ here referred to Himself as "the Son of man," a title which uniformly alludes to His self-abasement as the last Adam, or to some of the consequences of His obedience unto death.

As the result of Christ's atoning death, a new and living way has been opened into the very presence of God, blood-washed sinners having the title to draw near unto Him in full assurance of faith. But John 1:51, teaches something more than that the Redeemer is the uniting link between heaven and earth, the alone Mediator between God and men, namely that one of the precious fruits of His atoning work is the restoration of that long-forfeited intercourse between men and angels. As Christ broke down the middle wall of partition between Jews and Gentiles by His death upon the cross, having thereby slain the enmity which was between them, so He has also made an end of the estrangement which sin had caused between holy angels and men: they are brought together as the two branches of one family, gathered and united under one Head (Eph. 1:10). By the blood of His cross, Christ has reconciled all things in heaven and in earth (Col. 1:20), uniting them together in one happy fellowship, and for that reason did an angel say unto John, "I am thy fellowservant, and of thy brethren that have the testimony of Jesus" (Rev. 19:10). Thus John 1:51, teaches us that Christ is the Medium of a spiritual communion between the inhabitants of earth and heaven, the Maintainer of their fellowship.

Now as Christ announced the oneness which He would produce between the angels and His people by an allusion to Jacob's vision, so He referred to paradise as "Abraham's bosom" (Luke 16:22), and His apostle spoke of the new covenant (prefigured by Sarah) as "Jerusalem which is above is free, which is the mother of us all" (Gal. 4:26) and the New Testament saints as "the circumcision" (Phil. 3:3). In like manner (to return to Heb. 12:22), when he said "But ye are come unto mount Sion, and unto the city of the living God" he referred to the *spiritual* "Sion," or that blessed and glorious state into which believers have been called by the Gospel. That language looks back, of course, to the Old Testament, where (according to the different spellings in the Hebrew and Greek) it is called "Zion," and which represented or exemplified the highest revelation of Divine *grace* in Old Testament times. It was the place of God's habitation (Ps. 76:2). It was the object of God's special love, and the birthplace of His elect: "The Lord loveth the gates of Zion more than all the dwellings of Jacob. Glorious things are spoken of thee, O city of God. . . . And of Zion it shall be said, This and that man was born in her" (Ps. 87:2, 3, 5). Salvation and all blessings proceed therefrom (Ps. 128:5; 134:3).

Zion was not only the site of the temple, but the seat from which David reigned and ruled over the kingdom of Israel, issuing his laws and extending the power of his government over the whole of the holy land. As such it adumbrated the Messiah's kingdom. It is (in fulfilment of the Father's promise) to the *celestial* Zion that the Lord Jesus has been exalted (Ps. 2:6, and cf. Heb. 2:9), and there He sways His sceptre over the hearts of His people. Zion is where the spiritual David is enthroned, and whence "the rod of His strength" goes out, not only in bringing His redeemed into willing subjection, but by ruling "in the midst of His enemies" (Ps. 60:2; Isa. 2:3). Thus, in saying to believers of the Gospel, "Ye are come unto mount *Sion*, and unto the city of the living God," the Holy Spirit assures them that they have been given a personal interest in all the goodly things said of Sion anywhere in the Scriptures: that the spiritual content of those good things belongs to the New Testament saints particularly, that they have access to the spiritual throne of the antitypical David — the throne of grace. Since "all the promises of God in Him [Christ] are yea, and in Him Amen" (II Cor. 1:20), then those in Christ have a right and title to all the glorious things spoken of Zion in the Old Testament. Compare Joshua 1:5, and Hebrews 13: 5, 6, for an illustration of this principle.

There is another class of passages, somewhat different from those noticed above, which needs to be considered under this head of the spiritual import of verses in the Word. These may be suitably introduced by a statement in Revelation 11:8, "And their dead bodies shall lie in the street of the great city, *which spiritually is called* Sodom and Egypt, where also our Lord was crucified." As might well be expected, even by those who have only a comparatively slight acquaintance with the numerous works on the Apocalypse, with their manifold interpretations, commentators differ widely in their explanations of this verse. We do not propose to add to their number by attempting to identify the "two witnesses" or to determine if the "great city" where they are slain is to be understood literally or symbolically, nor whether the reference be to some place or some thing in the past, the present, or the future, for such speculations possess no practical value, offering not the slightest aid in fighting the good fight of faith. It is sufficient for our present purpose simply to call the reader's attention to the words we have italicized, and to point out how that clause establishes once more the principle of exegesis which we are here illustrating.

By saying that the "great city" of Revelation 11:8, is spiritually called Sodom and Egypt, the Holy Spirit intimates that it is characterized by the same evils which Scripture teaches us to associate with those places, that the filthiness of Sodom and the harshness of Egypt, in embittering the lives of God's people of old, marked the scene where the two witnesses testified for God and were slain for their fidelity. It is probable that the language of Revelation 11:8, contains a designed allusion to Ezekiel 16:44-59, where repeated mention is made of a mystical Sodom. "Mystical" we say, for when the Lord declared, "When I shall bring again their captivity, the captivity of Sodom and her daughters" (v. 53), and the question be asked whether there will yet be a restoring of the historical Sodom and the other cities of the plain, that is but to carnalize what is to be understood spiritually (by literalizing what is figurative), and would be to transfer the subject there spoken of from the moral government of God toward men, for the merely natural reign of the Divine providential arrangements respecting the material world.

When the Lord said to the inhabitants of Jerusalem, "Thou art thy mother's daughter, that lotheth her husband and her children . . . your mother was an Hittite, and your father an Amorite" (Ezek. 16:45), He was charging them with being guilty of the same abominations that marked the original dwellers in Palestine, who at a very early date apostatized from God, being among the first idolators after the great deluge. "As I live, saith the Lord God, Sodom thy sister hath not done, she nor her daughters, as thou hast done, thou and thy daughters. Behold, this was the iniquity of thy sister Sodom, pride, fulness of bread, and abundance of idleness" (16:48, 49). God spoke thus to the backslidden and corrupt Jewish nation because she trod the polluted way and imitated the sins of the ancient city of ill fame. To designate the covenant people "Sodom," because the state and manners of the one were identical with the other's, was one of the most solemn and impressive ways that could be taken to describe their inveterate depravity and vile character. Clear, then, it is that "Hittite," "Amorite" and "Sodom" in those verses are no more to be taken literally than is "David" in Ezekiel 34:23, or "Balaam" and "Jezebel" in Revelation 2:14, 20.

One more illustration of this kind must suffice. When His disciples asked Christ, "Why then say the scribes that Elias must first come?" He answered them, "Elias is come already," and we are told, "Then the disciples understood that He spake unto them of John the Baptist" (Matt. 17:10-13). That is one of the passages which Theosophists appeal to in support of their belief in reincarnation, and if our Lord's words are to be taken at their face value, then we should have to admit that they lend some color at least to that theory. Like the Dispensationalists of our day, the scribes were great sticklers for the letter of Scripture, and insisted that the Divine promise, "Behold, I will send you Elijah the prophet before the coming of the great and dreadful day of the Lord" (Mal. 4:5) meant just what it said. Here is certainly another case in point where the interpreter is needed, carefully to compare Scripture with Scripture and bring out the spiritual purport of them. That John the Baptist was *not* the actual person of the Tishbite is quite clear from his own blank denial, for when he was asked, "Art thou Elias?" he expressly declared, "I am not" (John 1:21). The question therefore remains, What did our Lord signify when He said of His forerunner *"Elias is come* already"?

That Christ was uttering a profound truth, one which could be apprehended only by spiritual and Divinely enlightened souls, when He declared that John the Baptist was Elijah, is very evident from His words to the apostles in Matthew 11:13, 14, "For all the prophets and the law were prophesied until John. And *if ye will receive it* [or "him"], this is Elias, which was for to come." Those words also contained an indirect rebuke of their carnal beliefs and sentiments respecting the expected kingdom of the Messiah: His added, "He that hath ears to hear, let him hear" (v. 15) confirms what we have just pointed out, for that call was never made except when something difficult for the natural man to understand was in view. John the Baptist was rejected by Israel's leaders. Herod had beheaded him, and Christ declared that He too should "suffer" (Matt. 17:12), and that was something which ill accorded with their views. A suffering Messiah, whose herald had been murdered, was difficult to harmonize with the teaching of the scribes concerning Malachi 4:5; yet there is nothing in that verse which should stumble us today, for our Lord has made its meaning quite clear.

In addition to the elucidation of Malachi 4:5, furnished above, it should be pointed out that the key passage which opens the mystery is Luke 1:17, where it was announced that John should go before Christ "in the spirit and power of Elias" — language which manifestly signifies that he was not a reincarnation of the Tishbite. The essential oneness of the two men in their character and work rendered the history of the earlier one a prophecy of the other. The latter appeared at a time when conditions were much the same as those which characterized the state of Israel in the days of Ahab. The resemblances between the two men are many and marked. John was essentially a preacher of repentance. He was a man of great austerity, garbed similarly to the prophet of Gilead. Real trial was made of his fidelity also by the hatred and persecution of the ungodly, but he was zealous for the Lord, both in reproving sin in high places and in seeking to bring about a reformation of his nation. Both his mission and his disposition were Elijah-like in character.

Ere leaving this branch of our many-sided subject, a much more numerous class of passages, which also differ considerably from those already noticed, require our attention, namely those which delineate the ups and downs of the Christian life. Many of them are set forth in plain and literal terms, others in highly figurative or typical language. Still others are concealed behind historical transactions which were Divinely designed to shadow forth the trials and temptations, the backslidings and falls, the conflicts and chastenings, the hopes and disappointments, the revivings and recoverings of saints in this era. We have left these until the last, not because they are of lesser importance, but because they require a Divinely taught and mature expositor to deal with them. They call for one who is well acquainted with his own heart, both with the workings of corruption and the operations of grace therein, as well as one with a considerable knowledge of God's "ways," if he is to trace out the different experiences of His people as they are reflected in the Scriptures. It is comparatively easy to bring out the spiritual meaning of, say, Exodus 15:23-25, or of Psalm 23; but it is harder (though necessary) to do so with Psalm 38:9, 10; 63:1, 2; 107:17-20; Proverbs 24:30-34; Isaiah 17:10, 11; and Hosea 2:14, 15.

Let us now illustrate from the history of Jonah as it spiritually portrays the experience of many a backslidden saint. The Lord gave that prophet a commandment, but it was contrary to his natural inclinations. He disobeyed, seeking to flee "from the presence of the Lord" — yielding to self-will saps the spirit of prayer and relish for the Word. Jonah went down into a ship — seeking the things of the world. God began to chasten him, by sending out "a great wind into the sea" because of his disobedience. That ought to have spoken loudly to his conscience, but, alas, he was sound asleep. Jonah perceived not the first manifestation of the Divine displeasure, and therefore was not troubled over the same. So it is with a backslidden saint: conscience slumbers when God afflicts: he is too stupefied to "hear the rod." But God would not allow Jonah to remain indifferent. He was rudely aroused from his slumbers by the shipmaster, lots were cast and it fell upon Jonah himself. His "cast me forth into the sea" (1:12) was the language of that despondency which comes upon one when he is made to reap the whirlwind. Yet God did not desert His wayward and despairing child: He "prepared a great fish to swallow up Jonah" — supernaturally preserving him. The sequel is blessed: said the erring one, "I cried by reason of mine affliction unto the Lord, and He heard me" (2:2); yes, and delivered him.

Such are, in their essential features, the usual experiences of a carnal believer who is determined to have his own way. In His lovingkindness the Lord disciplines such a one for his self-will and carnality. When he acts like "a bullock unaccustomed to the yoke" (Jer. 31:18), and follows a course of disobedience, God makes his self-pleasing plans to miscarry and prevents him reaching some Tarshish on which he set his heart. The Lord will not long suffer any of His own to do as they please. By the workings of His providence, a "great wind" comes and thwarts their desires and designs. If they fail to see God's hand therein and do not penitently humble themselves beneath it, then His rod falls still more heavily upon them. Then it is that they cry unto Him in their affliction. Note how Jonah looked beyond all instruments and acknowledged, "*Thou hast cast me into the deep*" (2:3) and owned his folly (2:8). In his "I will pay that that I have vowed" (2:9) we behold him restored to a spirit of submission; while his "salvation is of the Lord" freely ascribes his recovery unto His goodness. Thus Jonah 1 and 2 contain a spiritual picture both of the trials of a froward saint and of the faithfulness and mercy of God in His dealings with him.

16

THERE are certain types of mind, particularly the mystical and fanatical, which are prone to substitute fanciful concepts for spiritual interpretations. God's Word requires to be handled with reverential fear, and with much prayer for discernment and guidance, lest we tread on holy ground with the shoes of carnal wisdom; or the novice, striving after originality, give rein to his imagination, instead of disciplining himself to adhere strictly to the Analogy of Faith. Every preacher needs to be constantly on his guard against substituting human ingenuity for the teaching of the Spirit. Satan has ever mimicked the operations of the Spirit, and counterfeited a spiritual opening up of the Scriptures by wild perversions thereof. An early instance of this is the *Kabbala,* which, though of great esteem among the Jews, abounds in the most absurd explanations of Holy Writ. The rash allegorizing of Origen is another example to be studiously avoided, for he twisted the plainest and simplest texts into the most grotesque shapes or meanings. The strange system of exegesis adopted by Swedenborg is yet another case in point. The imagination needs to be bridled by both a tender conscience and the spirit of a sound mind.

Just so far as we really value a spiritual interpretation of God's Word will we abominate all counterfeits. Two extremes are to be guarded against, both by those who advance and those who receive some new explanation of a passage: a love of the fantastic and a prejudice against what is novel. There is a middle ground between hastily condemning or accepting, namely to weigh carefully and prayerfully what is presented, testing it by other passages and by our own experience. Doubtless most of us can recall some interpretations which were new, and which at first struck us as being "far-fetched," but which we now regard as sound and helpful. If the Holy Spirit had not informed us that Abraham's two wives were figures of the two covenants (Gal. 4:24), and that the words of Moses in Deuteronomy 30:11-14, were to be understood spiritually of the righteousness of faith (Rom. 10:6-9), we had considered such interpretations ridiculous. Remember that God grants light to one minister which He does not to another. Even though his explanation commend not itself to you at the moment, beware of rashly calling it "a perversion of the Scriptures," lest the same is being blessed to some poor child of God whose heart is feeding on what your head rejects.

22. *Double reference and meaning.* It is ever to be borne in mind that there is a fullness, as well as a depth, in the words of God which pertains not to those of men, so that rarely will a single and brief definition adequately explain a scriptural term. For that reason we must constantly be on our guard against limiting the scope of any Divinely inspired statement, and saying that it means only so and so. Thus, when

we are told that God made man in His own image and likeness, those words probably have at least a fourfold allusion. First, to the incarnation of the Son, for He is distinctly designated the "image of the invisible God" (Col. 1:15). Second, to man's being a tripartite creature, for "God said, Let us make man in our image" (Gen. 1:26) — a trinity in unity, consisting of "spirit and soul and body" (I Thess. 5:23). Third, in His moral likeness, which man lost at the fall, but which is restored at regeneration (Eph. 4:24; Col. 3:10). Fourth, to the position assigned man and the authority with which he was invested: "let them have dominion over" (Gen. 1:26). Adam was a "god" or ruler, under the Lord, of all mundane creatures.

In view of what has been pointed out, it is evident that the favorite dictum of Dispensationalists — "application is manifold, interpretation but one" — is erroneous, for the above are not four interpretations of the "image of God" from which we may choose, but the actual fourfold meaning of the term itself. To say that "interpretation is but one" is also flatly contradicted by our Lord's explanation of the parable of the sower, for when He defined its terms He gave three or four different significations to the "thorns" — compare Matthew 13:22; Mark 4:18, 19; Luke 8:14. We are in hearty accord with paragraph nine in the opening chapter of the Westminster Confession of Faith, when it says, "The infallible rule of interpretation of Scripture is the Scripture itself; and therefore, when there is a question about the true and full sense of any Scripture (which is not manifold, but one), it must be searched and known by other places that speak more clearly," except that we dissent from the limitation mentioned in the parentheses. We much prefer to side with Joseph Caryl (one of the framers of the Westminster Confession), who, when commenting on a verse the words of which were susceptible of various meanings, and which had been diversely explained by expositors, said, "In a Scripture which may, without the impeachment of any truth, admit divers sense, I would not be so positive in one as to reject all others."

Even if it were true that the grammatical meaning of a verse be only one, nevertheless it may have a double reference, as is certainly the case with some of the *prophecies* in Holy writ, which possess a major and a minor fulfilment. In his introduction to the book of Revelation in Ellicott's commentary, when writing upon prophecy, its annotator said, "The words of God mean more than one man or one school of thought can compass. There are depths of Truth unexplored which lie beneath the simplest sentences. Just as we are wont to say that history repeats itself, so the predictions of the Bible are not exhausted in one or even many fulfilments. Each prophecy is a single key which unlocks many doors, and the grand and stately drama of the Apocalypse has been played out perchance in one age to be repeated in the next." We greatly fear that it is nothing but narrowminded partisanship which has caused so many to disdain such a concept, and made them reject all other interpretations which accord not with their own particular system.

David said, "Thy commandment is exceeding broad" (Ps. 119:96): let us see to it that we do not contract or limit the same.

The Father's declaration concerning His Son "By His knowledge shall My righteous servant justify many" (Isaiah 53:11) certainly has a double force: the "knowledge" He possesses and the knowledge which He imparts. As Manton pointed out, "it may be taken either way: actively, for the knowledge which He shall give out; passively, for our apprehension of Christ," for the former without the latter cannot justify us. "By His knowledge" can be regarded both subjectively and objectively. First, by His own personal knowledge of the Father (John 17:25), which was the ground of what He imparted unto men (John 3:11) for their salvation. Second, for our saving knowledge of Him — received from Him. Instead of quibbling as to whether or not Isaiah intended to include each of those meanings, let us be thankful that he was guided to use language which included *both* senses. Again, our Lord's figurative expression when He declared that "the gates of hell" should not prevail against His Church" (Matt. 16:19) admits of a *double* reference: death Isa. 38:10) and the power of evil. Death and the grave *have prevailed* over every human institution, but not so over Christ (Acts 2:27), or His Church (Ps. 72:17; Matt. 28:20), nor shall any weapon formed against her prosper (Isa. 54:17) — meanings so dissimilar are no more surprising than the symbolical application of the word "lion" to Satan (I Peter 5:8) and to Christ (Rev. 5:5).

"Wherefore then serveth the law? It was added because of transgressions" (Gal. 3:19). That answer admits of two different significations. First, the immediate purpose in the Law's being formerly proclaimed and enforced subsequently to the promised inheritance to Abraham and his seed was to place a bridle upon the carnality of the Hebrews and check their sinning — by making known to them God's will and the fearful penalty of flouting His authority. Second, its ultimate design was to prepare the way for Christ, by demonstrating their need of Him because of their awful guilt. The "because of transgressions" is intentionally general enough to include both: to suppress transgressions, to make manifest transgressors. So too the next verse has a dual meaning: "Now a mediator is not a mediator of one [party] but God is one." In view of the context (v. 10 onwards, especially 16-19), "God is one" signifies first, that His purpose is *immutable*. His design was the same in both the Abrahamic and Sinaitic covenants — the Law being given with a gracious end in view, to pave the way for the Saviour: hence the question and answer in verse 21. Yet in view of the whole context it is equally clear, second, that "God is one" means that *His method of salvation* remains unaltered through all dispensations. "Is He the God of the Jews only? is He not also of the Gentiles? Yes, of the Gentiles also: seeing it is *one God*, which shall justify the circumcision by faith, and the uncircumcision through faith" (Rom. 3:29, 30).

What has just been noticed leads us to point out that the terms "Israel," "Jew," and "seed of Abraham" all have a twofold allusion. The expression "Israel after the flesh" (I Cor. 10:18) is obviously a dis-

criminating one, and would be meaningless were there no Israel after
the spirit, that is regenerated Israel, "the Israel of God" (Gal. 6:16). The
"Israel after the flesh" were the natural descendants of Abraham,
whereas the spiritual Israel, whether Jews or Gentiles, are those who are
born again and worship God in spirit and in truth. When the Psalmist
declared "Truly God is good to Israel, even to such as are of a clean
heart" (73:1), he certainly did not refer to the fleshly descendants of Jacob, for the greater part of them *lacked* "a clean heart"! When our Lord
said of Nathanael, "Behold an Israelite *indeed,* in whom is no guile"
(John 1:47), He obviously meant very much more than one who proceeded naturally from Jacob. His language was as distinguishing as
when He said, "If ye continue in My word, then are ye My disciples *indeed*" (John 8:31). "An Israelite indeed" connoted a genuine son of the
spiritual Israel, a man of faith and prayer, holy and honest. "In whom
is no guile" supplies further confirmation that a saved character was
there in view (compare Ps. 32:1).

When Christ said, "I am not sent but unto the lost sheep of the house
of Israel" (Matt. 15:24), He could not intend the fleshly descendants
of Jacob, for, as many Scriptures plainly show (Isa. 42:6; Rom. 15:
8, 9), He was sent unto the Gentiles also. No, the "lost sheep of the
house of Israel" there imported the whole election of grace. "And as
many as walk according to this rule, peace be on them, and mercy, and
upon the Israel of God" (Gal. 6:16) could not possibly refer to the nation,
for God's *wrath* was on *that* — it is on the Israel chosen by the Father, redeemed by the Son and regenerated by the Spirit that Divine peace and
mercy rest. "Not as though the word of God had taken none effect. For
they are not all Israel, which are of Israel" (Rom. 9:6). The Jews er-
roneously imagined that the promises which God had made to Abraham
and his seed pertained only to his natural descendants: hence their
claim "we have Abraham to our father" (Matt. 3:9). But those promises
were not made to men after the flesh, but to men after the spirit, the
regenerate, they alone being the "children of the promise" (Rom. 9:8).
God's promises to Abraham, Isaac and Jacob were given to them *as believers,* and they are the spiritual property and food of believers, and
none else (Rom. 4:13, 16). Until that fact be grasped, we shall be all
at sea with the Old Testament promises (cf. II Cor. 1:20, and 7:1; II
Peter 1:4).

"Know ye therefore that they which are of faith, the same are the children of Abraham" (Gal. 3:7). The children of Abraham are of two kinds,
physical and spiritual: those who are his by nature, and those who are
connected with him by grace. "To be the children of a person in a
figurative sense is equivalent to 'resemble him and to be involved in his
fate,' good or bad. To be 'the children of God' is to be like God, and
also, as the apostle states, it is to be 'heirs of God.' To be 'the children
of Abraham' is to resemble Abraham, to imitate his conduct and to share
his blessedness" (John Brown). So to be " the children of the wicked
one" (Matt. 13:38) is to be conformed to his vile image, both in character and in conduct (John 8:44), and to share his doom (Matt. 15:41).

Christ said to the carnal Jews of His day, "If ye were Abraham's children, ye would do the works of Abraham" (John 8:39). It is his
spiritual children who "walk in the steps of that faith which he had"
(Rom. 4:12) and who are "blessed with faithful Abraham" (Gal. 3:9).
We must be united to Christ, who is *the Son* of Abraham" (Matt. 1:1),
in order to enter into the blessings which God covenanted unto the
patriarch. The double significance of the expression "children" or "seed
of Abraham" was plainly intimated at the beginning, when God likened
his seed to the stars of the heavens and the sand which is upon the sea
shore (Gen. 22:17).

In like manner, the word "Jews" is applied to two very different classes
of people, though few today would think so if they confined themselves
to the ministry of a class who pride themselves on having more light than
the majority of professing Christians. Nevertheless, such is uniquivocally
established by the declaration of Romans 2:28, 29: "For he is not a Jew,
which is one outwardly; neither is that circumcision, which is outward
in the flesh: But he is a Jew, which is one inwardly; and circumcision is
that of the heart, in the spirit, and not in the letter; whose praise is not of
men, but of God." Surely nothing could be plainer than that, and in the
light of such a statement it seems passing strange that there are those —
boasting loudly of their orthodoxy, and bitterly condemning all who differ from them — who insist that the term "Jew" pertains only to the natural descendants of Jacob, and ridicule the idea that there is any such
thing as a spiritual Jew. But when God tells us, "he is a Jew, which is
one *inwardly*," He manifestly means that the true "Jew," the antitypical
one, is a regenerated person, who enjoys the "praise" or approbation of
God.

It is not only childish, but misleading, to affirm that "Israel" means
Israel and "Jew" means *Jew,* and that when God's Word makes mention
of Jerusalem or Zion nothing else is referred to than those actual places.
Those who make such assertions are but deceiving themselves (and
others who are gullible enough to heed them) by the mere *sound* of
words. As well aver that "flesh" signifies nothing more than the physical
body, that "water" (John 4:14) refers only to that material element, or
that "death" (John 5:24) signifies nothing but physical dissolution.
There is an end of all *interpretation* — bringing out the *sense* of Scripture — when such a foolish attitude be adopted. Each verse calls for
careful and prayerful study, so that it may be fairly ascertained *which*
the Spirit has in view: the carnal Israel or the spiritual, the literal seed
of Abraham or the mystical, the natural Jew or the regenerate, the earthly
Jerusalem or the heavenly, the typical Zion or the antitypical. God has
not written His Word in such a way that the average reader is made independent of that help which He has designed to give through His ac-
credited teachers.

We can well imagine those of our readers who have sat under the
errors of Dispensationalism saying, "All of this seems very confusing, for
we have been taught to distinguish sharply between Israel and the
Church, the one being an earthly people and the other a heavenly." Of

course, Israel was an "earthly people": so too were the Egyptians, the Babylonians, and all the other inhabitants of this world. This writer and his Christian readers are also an "earthly people," for neither their bodies nor their souls have yet been removed to heaven. In reply, the objector will say that it was Israel's *inheritance* which was an earthly one. But we ask, was it? Was the inheritance of the patriarchs an earthly one? Hebrews 11:14-16, plainly shows otherwise, for there we are told "they seek a country," that after they had entered the land of Canaan "now they [Abraham, Isaac and Jacob] desire a better country, that is, an heavenly." Was the inheritance of Moses an earthly one? Let Hebrews 11:26, make answer: "Esteeming the reproach of Christ greater riches than the treasures in Egypt: for he had respect unto the recompence of the reward," namely the eternal one (cf. Col. 3:24)! Was David's inheritance a mundane one? If so, how could he speak of himself as "a stranger in the earth" (Ps. 39:12; 119:119)? Psalm 73:25 shows what his heart was set upon.

It is not sufficient to affirm that Israel's inheritance was an earthly one: *which* "Israel" must be definitely stated, and also what the inheritance adumbrated. As the portion which Jehovah appointed, promised, and gave to Abraham and his descendants, that land of Canaan has, throughout the Christian era, been rightly regarded as figuring the heavenly inheritance, to which the members of Christ are journeying as they pass through this scene of sin and trial. In order to obtain the complete typical picture of the varied spiritual experiences and exercises of God's elect as they were so vividly foreshadowed of old, we have to take into account not only the history of the Hebrews in Egypt and their wilderness journeyings, but also what was demanded of them in order to make their entrance into and occupation of the land of Canaan. As we have so frequently pointed out in our articles on the life and times of Joshua, Canaan is also to be contemplated from *two standpoints,* natural and spiritual: spiritually, as portraying the heritage of regenerated Israelites, which heritage is to be appropriated and enjoyed now by faith and obedience, but which will not be fully entered into until the Jordan of death has been crossed. Admittedly, great care has to be taken with the Analogy of Faith.

Though Canaan was a divine gift to the natural Israel, nevertheless their occupation thereof was the result of their own prowess. It was indeed bestowed upon them by free gift from God, yet it had to be conquered by them. Therein was accurately shadowed forth what is necessary in order to make an entrance into the heavenly Canaan. The book of Joshua not only displays the sovereign grace of God, exhibits His covenant faithfulness, and the mighty power which He puts forth on behalf of His people, but it also makes known what He required from them in the discharge of their responsibility, and shows that the Lord only fought for His people while they remained in entire dependence on and were in complete subjection to Him. There were formidable obstacles to be surmounted, fierce and powerful foes to be vanquished, a hard and protracted warfare to be waged, and only while they *actively concurred* did the Lord show Himself strong on their behalf. "For *if* ye shall diligently keep all these commandments which I command you, to do them, to love the Lord your God, to walk in His ways, and to cleave unto Him; then will the Lord drive out all these nations. . . . Every place whereon the soles of your feet shall tread shall be yours" (Deut. 11:22-24). That was not the "if" of uncertainty, but had to do with their accountability — as the "if" of John 8:31, 51; Colossians 1:23 and Hebrews 3:6, 14 has to do with ours.

The Church's inheritance is wholly of divine grace and mediatorial purchase, yet it is not entered into by the heirs of promise without arduous efforts on their part. There is the strait gate to be entered and the narrow way to be trodden (Matt. 6:13, 14). There is a race to be run which calls for temperance in all things (I Cor. 9:24-26). There is a fight to be fought (I Tim. 6:12; II Tim. 4:7), and in order to be successful therein we have to take unto us "the whole armor of God" (Eph. 6:13) and make daily use of the same. There is a ceaseless conflict with the flesh to be engaged in (Gal. 5:17), a Devil to be steadfastly resisted in the faith (I Peter 5:8, 9), an alluring and opposing world to be overcome (James 4:4; I John 5:4). While it is blessedly true that "we which have believed *do enter* into rest" (Heb. 4:3). Christ's yoke is taken upon us, nevertheless the divine injunction remains, "let us *labor* therefore to *enter* into that rest" (Heb. 4:11) which awaits us on high, and of which the land flowing with milk and honey was the emblem.

17

23. *The law of order.* God's Word is like His works: designed disposition and minute precision characterizing it throughout. If "to every thing there is a season, and a time to every purpose under heaven" (Eccles. 3:1) in the natural world, assuredly the same holds good in connection with the spiritual realm and all that pertains thereto. Even those who make no claim to being Christians recognize and acknowledge that "order is heaven's first law." God is a God of order, and most unmistakably is that fact displayed all through Holy Writ. Everything therein is methodically arranged and in its proper place: change that arrangement and confusion and error at once ensue. Thus it is of deep importance that we pay close attention to *the order* in which Truth has been set forth by the omniscient Spirit. The key to many a verse is to be found in noting the position it occupies, its coherence with what precedes, its relation to what follows.

Whether its contents be considered historically, doctrinally, or typically, Genesis must open the Word, for it is the book of *beginnings*. It has been aptly called "the seed-plot of the Bible," for in it is to be found in germ form almost everything which is afterwards more fully developed in the books which follow. Doctrinally, its theme is that of Divine election, which is the *first* act of God's grace unto His people. Then comes Exodus, which treats of redemption by purchase and power (6: 6; 15:13). The third book, as might be expected, views God's people as on resurrection ground, being not so much doctrinal as experiential in its character. Leviticus shows what we are redeemed unto, having for its theme fellowship and worship: its key is hung on the door — the Lord speaking out of the tabernacle (1:1). The fourth book deals with the practical side of the spiritual life, tracing out the history of the believer in this world — for four is the number of the earth. "The wilderness" (1:1) is a symbol of the world in its fallen condition, the place of testing and trial. It subject is the walk and warfare of the saints.

The positioning of those four books clearly manifests *design* in the Divine workmanship, and teaches us the order in which the Truth should be presented. An equally striking illustration is seen in the juxtaposition and order of the last two books of Solomon, for the theme of Ecclesiastes is unquestionably: "No satisfaction to be found under the sun," while that of the Canticles tells of "full satisfaction in the Son": over the one may be inscribed: "Whosoever drinketh of this water [the cisterns of the world] shall thirst again"; over the other: "But whosoever drinketh of the water that I shall give him shall never thirst" (John 4:14). In II Timothy 3:16, Paul informs us that the Scriptures are profitable "for doctrine, for reproof, for correction, for instruction in righteousness," and that is the very *order* which he has followed in his epistles. For

Romans is a doctrinal treatise, the Corinthian epistles a reproof of disorders in the assembly, Galatians a correcting of erroneous teaching, and Ephesians describes that walk which alone is worthy of a child of God.

Not only are the books in the Bible unerringly positioned, but the contents of each are arranged in logical and necessary sequence. Thus it is intensely interesting to mark how that each of the patriarchs in Genesis shadowed forth some distinct and fundamental truth concerning the believer. In Abraham we have illustrated that of Divine election and effectual calling. In Isaac we have portrayed Divine sonship (by a supernatural birth) and the life of submission to God's will. In Jacob we have pictured the conflict between the flesh and the spirit: the two natures in the believer, intimated by his dual name, Jacob — Israel. In Joseph we have exemplified the grand truth of heirship: following a season of trial, made ruler of Egypt. Thus the historical order is also the doctrinal and experiential, progressive and climacteric. The five great offerings of Leviticus 1–5 typify as many distinct aspects of the person and work of the Lord Jesus, and invaluable instruction is to be obtained by pondering the sequence of them.

Psalms 22, 23, and 24 present us with a significant and blessed triad, especially as Christ is seen in them. In the first, we behold Him suffering for His people; in the last we see Him as the King of glory receiving a royal welcome into heaven, and are furnished with a delineation of the characteristics possessed by those whom He fits to dwell with Him there; while in the central one we are shown how graciously He ministers to and provides for His sheep (whom He is leading to the celestial fold) during the interval they are left on earth. In Psalm 22 we behold the "good Shepherd" (John 10:11), in 23 the "great Shepherd" (Heb. 13:20), in 24 the "chief Shepherd" (I Peter 5:4). Again, if it be essential to the believer's comfort that, finding Romans 7 accurately describes his spiritual experience, his faith should lay hold of the Divine assurances of Romans 8, it is equally necessary that preachers not only hold fast to the absolute sovereignty of God in election and reprobation as set forth in Romans 9; but that they also proclaim the free offer of the Gospel to all men and enforce their responsibility to accept that offer, as presented in Romans 10.

What has been exemplified in the above paragraphs applies not only in the general, but is equally true in detail. For example, *the arrangement* of the ten commandments of the moral law (which comprehend the sum of righteousness) is profoundly significant. They were written on two tables of stone, to intimate that they fall into two distinct groups. The first four concern our responsibility *Godward*, the last six of our obligations *manward*. Vain is it to pretend that we are sincere worshippers of God if the duties of love unto our neighbors be neglected; equally worthless is that profession of piety which, while abstaining from crimes against our fellows, withholds from the Majesty of heaven the honor and glory which are His due. Again, the five exhortations contained in Psalm 37:1-7 are arranged in logical and inevitable order. We must cease from fretfulness and envy if we would trust in the Lord, and we must trust in Him before we can delight in Him, and that is necessary in order to have a confident committing of our way unto Him, and resting in and waiting patiently for Him.

The *order* of the beatitudes in Matthew 5:3-11, is full of valuable instruction, and we miss much by failing to attend closely thereto. In the first four we are shown the heart-exercises of those who have been awakened by the Spirit. First, there is a sense of need, a realization of their nothingness and emptiness. Second, there is a judging of self, a consciousness of guilt and sorrowing over their lost condition. Third, an end of attempting to justify themselves, an abandonment of all pretences to personal merit, a taking of their place in the dust before God. Fourth, the eye of the soul is turned away from self to Another: they are conscious of their dire need of salvation. The next four describe the fruits found in the regenerate. Thus, in those beatitudes Christ gives the distinguishing birthmarks of those who are the subjects of His kingdom, and makes known the ones on whom God's benediction rests.

What anointed eye can fail to see the perfect order of the model prayer Christ has given His disciples? In it He has supplied a simple but comprehensive directory: revealing how God is to be approached by His children, the order in which their requests are to be presented, the things they most need to ask for, and the homage due unto Him. Every aspect of prayer is included: adoration, supplication, argumentation. Every clause in it occurs in the Old Testament, denoting that our prayers must be scriptural if they are to be acceptable (I John 5:14). Its petitions are seven in number, showing the completeness of the outline here furnished. All its pronouns are in the plural, teaching the Christian that the needs of his brethren and sisters, and not merely his own, should be before him when he bows at the throne of grace.

Let the student pay close attention to the order followed in these additional examples, which we leave him to work out for himself. The miracles of Christ in Matthew 8 and 9. The seven parables in Matthew 13. The sevenfold result of justification as set forth in Romans 5:1-11. The seven graces of II Peter 1:5-7, the presence and cultivation of which enables the saint to make his calling and election sure both to himself and his fellows, for the "these things" of verse 10 are those mentioned in verses 5-7. Everything in Scripture is according to definite design.

The special design of Luke was to set forth the perfections of our Lord's humanity, and it is very blessed to trace out the different passages in his Gospel where Christ is seen as *a Man of prayer*. "It came to pass, that Jesus also being baptized, and praying, the heaven was opened" (3:21). Luke is the only one who supplies this significant detail, and a most precious one it is. The Saviour's baptism marked the end of His private life, and the beginning of His official mission. And here we learn that He was in the act of devotion at the very outset of His public ministry. He was engaged in dedicating Himself unto God, seeking grace for the stupendous work that lay before Him. Thus the first sight which the multitude had of Him was in prayer! "And He withdrew Himself into the wilderness, and prayed" (v. 16). This oc-

(5:16)

curred just after His miracles of mercy, when there went "a fame abroad of Him: and great multitudes came together to hear, and to be healed by Him." His response to this show of popularity was striking, and full of instruction for His servants. He retired from the acclaims of the masses, and got alone with God. Again, "He went out into a mountain to pray, and continued all night in prayer to God" (6:12). This followed immediately after the scribes and Pharisees were "filled with madness" against Him, and right before He selected the twelve. Our Redeemer made no attempt to fight His enemies, but retired to commune with the Father. Before calling the apostles, He spent the night petitioning God.

"And it came to pass, as He was alone praying, His disciples were with Him: and He asked them saying, Whom say the people that I am?" (9:18). This was just following His feeding of the multitude: after engaging in public duty, He withdrew in order to have private devotion. We may infer from the question which He asked His disciples that the unbelief of men was beginning to cast a shadow upon His soul, and that He now sought relief and strength from above. "And went up into the mountain to pray. And as He prayed, the fashion of His countenance was altered, and His raiment was white and glistening" (9:28, 29). It was while engaged in prayer that Christ was transfigured — how significant, and instructive! "And it came to pass, that, as He was praying in a certain place, when He ceased, one of His disciples said unto Him, Lord, teach us to pray" (11:1). This is one of the passages (see also the Messianic Psalms) which gives us some insight into the nature of His supplications. As they heard *Him*, the disciples felt they knew nothing about prayer! "And the Lord said, Simon, Somon . . . I have prayed for thee, that thy faith fail not" (22:31, 32). There we behold Him as the great High Priest making intercession for one of His own. And He "kneeled down and prayed, saying, Father, if Thou be willing, remove this cup from Me: nevertheless, not My will, but Thine, be done" (22:41, 42). There is the climax of prayer: complete surrender to and acquiescence in the Divine will.

In the seven miracles recorded in John's Gospel we may discern a striking order of thought as they portray Christ communicating *life* to His people. In His turning of the water into wine at the Cana marriage feast (2:6-11) we are shown, symbolically, our *need of life* — Christ supplying what was lacking. In the healing of the nobleman's son (4:47-54), who was "at the point of death," we have pictured the *bestowment* of life. In the healing of the impotent man (5:3-9) we behold the *power* of life, enabling a helpless cripple to rise up and walk. In the feeding of the multitude (6:11) we see how graciously Christ *sustains* our life. In His going to the fearful disciples on the storm-swept sea we witness Him *defending* their lives, delivering them from danger. In the response made by the blind man whose eyes Christ opened (9:7, 38) we learn what is to be *the occupation* of life — he worshipped Him: in this way, supremely, we are to employ the new nature. In the raising of

Lazarus from the sepulchre (11:44) we have the consummation of life, for the resurrection of the saints is the prelude to their eternal felicity.

The teaching of our Lord concerning the Holy Spirit's operations within and toward the saints follows an instructive and a climacteric order. First, He made mention of being "born of the Spirit" (3:6, 8), for *quickening* is His initial operation upon the elect. Second, by means of figurative language (cf. 3:5), He spoke of the Spirit's *indwelling*: "the water that I shall give him shall be in him a well of water springing up into everlasting life" (4:14). Third, He declared that there should be a *breaking forth* of the same, and a refreshing of others: "out of his belly [or innermost part] shall flow rivers of living water. But this spake He of the Spirit" (7:38, 39). Fourth, He promised that the blessed Spirit should be theirs *permanently*: "I will pray the Father, and He shall give you another Comforter, that He may abide with you for ever" (14:16). Fifth, He announced that the Spirit would fully *instruct them*: "He shall teach you all things" (14:26). Sixth, He declared that the Spirit should both testify of Him and equip them to *testify unto Him*: "But when the Comforter is come, whom I will send unto you from the Father, even the Spirit of truth, which proceedeth from the Father, He shall testify of Me: and ye also shall bear witness" (15:26, 27). Seventh, Christ asserted that the Spirit should *magnify Him*: "He shall glorify Me: for He shall receive of Mine, and shall show it unto you" (14:14), making Me altogether lovely in your eyes.

18

24. *The law of cause and effect.* By this we mean the observing and tracing out of *the connection* which exists between certain notable events in the life of an individual or nation and what led up to the same. For instance, the closing events recorded in the sad history of Lot startle and stagger us by their deplorable and revolting nature; yet if we carefully ponder all that preceded, then the tragic finale can almost be anticipated. Or take the better-known case of Simon Peter's denial of Christ, which seems to be altogether out of keeping with what we know of his character. Strange indeed is the anomaly presented: that the one who feared not to step out of the ship and walk on the sea to his beloved Master, and who boldly drew his sword and smote off the ear of the high priest's servant when a strong force came to arrest the Saviour, should tremble in the presence of a maid, and be afraid to own the Lord Jesus! Nevertheless, his melancholy fall was not an isolated event having no relation to what had gone before: rather was it all of a piece with his previous attitude and actions, being the logical, and virtually the inevitable, sequel to them. These are examples of a numerous class of cases, and they should be carefully borne in mind as we read the biographical portions of Scripture.

This principle of interpretation will be the more easily grasped when we point out that it is much the same as the law of sowing and reaping. That law operates now, in this world, and it is an important part of the expositor's task to observe its outworking in the lives of biblical characters. Consider then some of the details recorded about Lot *before* his career ended amid the dark shadows of his mountain cave. After the initial reference to him in Genesis 11:31, nothing is said about him until after Abraham's sorry sojourn in Egypt. It appears that Lot contracted Egypt's spirit and acquired a taste for its fleshpots. In Genesis 13:6, 7, we read of a strife between the herdsmen of Abraham and Lot: the Lord's later rewarding of the former and the subsequent conduct of the latter seem clearly to intimate which of them was to blame. The proposal that Abraham made to his nephew (13:8, 9) was a most generous one, and Lot's carnality at once appeared in the advantage he took of it. Instead of leaving the choice to his uncle, Lot yielded to the lust of the eyes, and chose the plain of Jordan, which was well watered and "like the land of Egypt"! Next, he "pitched his tent toward Sodom" (13:12). Then he went and "dwelt in Sodom" (14:12), forsaking the pilgrim's tent for a "house" (19:3). There he settled down, became an alderman, sitting in its "gate" (19:1), while his daughters married men of Sodom.

Let us in a similar way briefly trace the several downward steps which led to Peter's awful fall. There was first his self-assurance and proud boast when he declared, "Although all shall be offended, yet will

109

not I" (Mark 14:29). We doubt not his sincerity on that occasion, but it is clear that he realized not his instability. Self-ignorance and self-confidence ever accompany each other; not until self be really known is it distrusted. Second, he failed to comply with his Master's exhortation, "watch ye and pray" (Mark 14:38-40), and instead went to sleep again — it is only a felt sense of weakness which causes one earnestly to seek strength. Third, he disregarded Christ's solemn warning that Satan desired to seize and sift him (Luke 22:31, 33). Fourth, we behold him acting in the energy of the flesh in drawing the sword (John 18:10). Naturally, he meant well, but spiritually, how dull his perceptions: how completely out of place was his weapon in the presence of the meek and lowly Saviour! No wonder we are next told that he followed Christ "afar off" (Matt. 26:58), for he was entirely out of the current of His spirit. Solemn is it to see him disregarding the providential warning of the closed door (John 18:16). He was cold spiritually as well as physically, but how pathetic to see him warming himself at the enemy's fire (John 18:18). That he "sat down" in such circumstances (Mark 14:54) shows how serious was his decline. All of these things paved the way for his ultimate cursing and swearing (Matt. 26:74).

What unmistakable and manifest instances are the above of the working of the law of cause and effect! But let us turn now to a different class of cases, where there was a different sowing and a happier reaping. In Genesis 22 we have one of the most touching and exquisite scenes presented in the Scriptures. There we behold grace triumphing over nature, the spirit rising superior to the flesh. It was the final and severest test to which the faith and obedience of Abraham were submitted. He was called upon to sacrifice his beloved Isaac, and to be himself the executioner. How grandly the sorely tried patriarch responded, binding his only son, laying him on the altar, taking the knife in his hand, and desisting not until a voice from heaven bade him slay not the lad. Now observe the blessed though less-known sequel. Said the angel of the covenant unto him, "By Myself have I sworn, saith the Lord, for *because* thou hast done this thing, and hast not withheld thy son, thine only son: That in blessing I will bless thee, and in multiplying I will multiply thy seed . . . *because* thou hast obeyed My voice" (vv. 16-18). Thus was the Lord pleased to make mention of His servant's submission as the consideration of His gracious reward on this occasion: not that there was any proportion between the one and the other, but that He thereby placed this honor upon that faith and obedience by which Abraham had honored Him. Later, he made gracious promises to Isaac "because that Abraham obeyed My voice, and kept My charge" (26:2-5).

In Numbers 14 a very different scene is presented to our view. There we behold the reactions of Israel unto the doleful report made by the unbelieving majority of the spies which Moses had sent to reconnoiter Canaan. "All the congregation lifted up their voice, and . . . wept," conducting themselves like a lot of peevish children. Worse still, they murmured against Moses and Aaron, and spoke of appointing a new leader to conduct them back again to Egypt. At considerable risk to their lives (v. 10), Joshua and Caleb remonstrated with them. The Lord interposed, passed sentence upon that faithless generation, sentencing them to die in the wilderness. In blessed contrast therewith, He said, "But My servant Caleb, *because* he had another spirit with him, and hath followed Me fully, him will I bring into the land whereinto he went; and his seed shall possess it" (v. 24). Numbers 25 supplies us with another example of the same principle. Setting aside his own feelings, the son of Eleazar acted for the honor of Jehovah, and of him the Lord said, he "hath turned My wrath away from the children of Israel, while he was zealous for My sake. . . . Wherefore say, Behold, I give unto him My covenant of peace: and he shall have it, and his seed after him, even the covenant of an everlasting priesthood; *because* he was zealous for his God, and made an atonement for the children of Israel" (vv. 10-13).

Now it scarcely needs pointing out that neither Abraham, Caleb, nor Phinehas brought God into his debt, or placed Him under any obligation to them. Yet their cases illustrate a most important principle in the governmental ways of God. That principle is stated in His own declaration: "them that honor Me. I will honor, and they that despise Me shall be lightly esteemed" (I Sam. 2:30). Though there be nothing whatever meritorious about the good works of His people, God is pleased to bear testimony of His approval of the same and make it manifest concerning His commandments that "in keeping of them there is great reward" (Ps. 19:11). Thus the Lord witnessed to His acceptance of the holy zeal of Phinehas by putting an immediate stop to the plague upon Israel, and by entailing the priesthood on his family. As Matthew Henry pointed out, "The reward answered to the service: by executing justice he had made an atonement for the children of Israel (v. 13), and therefore he and his should henceforth be employed in making atonement by sacrifice." Proverbs 11:31, states the same principle, "Behold, the righteous shall be recompensed in the earth." As Spurgeon remarked, "Albeit that the dispositions of Divine grace are to the fullest degree sovereign and irrespective of human merit, yet in the dealings of Providence there is often discernible a rule of justice by which the injured are at length avenged and the righteous ultimately delivered."

David acknowledged, "The Lord recompensed me according to my righteousness, according to the cleanness of my hands in His eyesight" (Ps. 18:24). He was alluding to God's delivering him from his enemies, particularly from Saul. How had he conducted himself toward the king? Did he commit any sin which warranted his hostility? Did he injure him in any way? No, he neither hated Saul nor coveted his throne, and therefore that monarch was most unjust in so relentlessly seeking his life. So innocent was David in this respect that he appealed to the great Searcher of hearts: "Let not them that are mine enemies *wrongfully* rejoice over me" (Ps. 35:19). Thus, when he said, "The Lord recompense me according to my righteousness" he was far from giving vent to a pharisaical spirit. Instead, he was avowing his innocence before the bar of *human* equity. Since he bore his persecutor no malice, he enjoyed the testimony of a good conscience. In all that he suffered at the hand of Saul, David retaliated not: he not only refused to slay, or even injure, him when he was at his mercy, but he took every opportunity to serve the cause of Israel, nowithstanding the ingratitude, envy and treachery he received in return. In his deliverance and in having the throne conferred upon him, David recognized one of the basic principles operating in the Divine government of this world, and owned that God had graciously rewarded him because of his integrity.

Deity hesitates not to take as one of His titles "the Lord God of recompences" (Jer. 51:56), and has shown, all through His Word, that He deals with sinner and saint as such. Unto Joshua He said that if he gave His Word its proper place, meditated in it day and night, that he might observe to do according to all that is written therein, "*then* thou shalt make thy way prosperous, and *then* thou shalt have good success" (1:8, and cf. Job 36:11; Prov. 3:1-4). On the other hand, He said to wayward Israel "Why transgress ye the commandments of the Lord, that ye cannot prosper? *because* ye have forsaken the Lord, He hath also forsaken you" (II Chron. 24:20). That is an unvarying principle in His government. Of Uzziah we read, "as long as he sought the Lord, God made him to prosper" (II Chron. 26:5). The judgment of God even upon Ahab's kingdom was postponed "because he humbled himself before Me" said God (I Kings 21:29). Contrariwise, He told David that the sword should never depart from his house "because thou hast despised Me" (II Sam. 12:9, 10). The New Testament teaches the same thing. "Blessed are the merciful: for they shall obtain mercy" (Matt. 5:7). "If ye forgive not men their trespasses, neither will your Father forgive your trespasses" (6:15); "with what measure ye mete, it shall be measured to you again" (7:2). "*Because* thou hast kept the word of My patience, *I also* will keep thee" (Rev. 3:10).

God has established an inseparable connection between holiness and happiness, and it is no small part of the expositor's work to point out that as our ways please Him His smile is upon us; but when we are wayward, we are greatly the losers; to show that though God's people are not under the curse of the rod they *are* under its discipline; and for him to note scriptural illustrations of that fact. It is one thing to have our sins pardoned, but it is quite another to enjoy God's favors in providence and nature as well as spiritually, as the lives of biblical characters clearly exemplify. God does not afflict willingly (Lam. 3:33), but chastens because we give Him occasion to do so (Ps. 89:30-33). When we grieve not the Holy Spirit, He makes Christ more real and precious to the soul; the channel of blessing is unchoked, and real answers are received to prayer. But alas, how often we give God occasion to say "your sins have withholden good things from you" (Jer. 5:25). Then let the preacher miss no opportunity of proving from Scripture that the path of obedience is the path of blessing (Ps. 81:11-16), and demonstrate that God orders His ways with us according to our conduct (Isa. 48:10) — He did so with Christ Himself (John 8:29; 10:17; Ps. 45:7).

25. *The law of emphasis.* The fundamental importance and perpetuity of the moral law was intimated in its being written by God's own finger, and by the two tables on which it was inscribed being placed for safe custody within the sacred ark. The inestimable value of the Gospel was signified in its being announced to the shepherds by an angel, "Behold, I bring you good tidings of great joy, which shall be to all people," and his being joined by a great multitude of the heavenly host praising God, and saying, "Glory to God in the highest, and on earth peace, good will toward men" (Luke 2:10, 14). The relative weightiness of anything is generally indicated by the place and prominence given to it in the Scriptures. Thus, only two of the evangelists make mention of the actual birth of Christ; only one of them supplies us with any details about His boyhood; Mark and Luke alone refer to His ascension; but all four of them describe His sacrificial death and victorious resurrection! How plainly that tells us *which* should be most pressed by His servants, and which should most engage the hearts and minds of His people!

Another means and method employed by the Spirit to arrest our attention and focus our minds upon distinct portions of the Truth is His use of a great number of "figures of speech." In them He has arranged words and phrases in an unusual manner for the purpose of more deeply impressing the reader with what is said. The learned author of *The Companion Bible* (now almost unobtainable) dealt more fully with this subject than any English writer, and from him we now select one or two examples. The figure of *anabasis* or graduation, in which there is the working up to a climax, as in "Who shall lay any thing to the charge of God's elect? It is God that justifieth. Who is he that condemneth? It is Christ that died, *yea rather,* that is risen again, who is *even* at the right hand of God, who *also* maketh intercession for us" (Rom. 8:33, 34). So again in II Peter 1:5-7, "add to your faith virtue . . . charity." The opposite figure is that of *catabasis* or gradual descent, a notable instance of which is found in Philippians 2:6-8.

The more common form of emphasis is that of *repetition.* This is found in the Word in quite a variety of ways, as in the doubling of a name: "Abraham, Abraham" (Gen. 22:11). There were six other individuals whom the Lord thus addressed: "Jacob, Jacob" (46:2), "Moses, Moses" (Exod. 3:4), "Samuel, Samuel" (I Sam. 3:10), "Martha, Martha" (Luke 10:41), "Simon, Simon" (22:10), "Saul, Saul" (Acts 9:4). Then there was our Lord's pathetic "O Jerusalem, Jerusalem" (Matt. 23:37), and His cry of anguish, "My God, My God" (Matt. 27:46); as there will yet be the urgent "Lord, Lord" of the lost (Luke 13:25). Such intensified forms of expression as "the holy of holies," "the song of songs," "vanity of vanities," and the unspeakable "for ever and ever," express the same principle. Again, "Wait on the Lord: be of good courage, and He shall strengthen thine heart: wait, I say, on the Lord" (Ps. 27:14); "Rejoice in the Lord alway: and again I say, Rejoice" (Phil. 4:4). Yet more emphatic is the "holy, holy, holy" of Isaiah 6:3, the "O earth, earth, earth, hear the word of the Lord" (Jer. 22:29), and because it will not, the "I will overturn, overturn, overturn" (Ezek. 21:27), with the resultant "Woe, woe, woe, to the inhabitants of the earth" (Rev. 8:13).

A simple form of structural repetition occurs in the adoring language found at both the beginning and the end of Psalm 8, "O Lord our Lord, how excellent is Thy name in all the earth!" Other forms of this principle are what are technically known as *cyloides*, or circular repetition, where the same phrase occurs at regular intervals, as in "Turn us again, O God" (Ps. 80:3, 7, 9); *epibole*, or overlaid repetition, where the same phrase is used at irregular intervals, as "the voice of the Lord" (Ps. 29: 3, 4, 5, 7, 8, 9); *epimone*, or lingering, where the repetition is with the design of making a more lasting impression, as in John 21:15-17, where our Lord continued to challenge the love of His erring disciple, and evinced His acceptance of his responses by His "feed My lambs, feed My sheep."

In the Old Testament many examples are found of what is called Hebrew parallelism, in which the same thought is expressed in different language. For instance, "He shall judge the world in righteousness, He shall minister judgment to the people in uprightness" (Ps. 9:8). Pride goeth before destruction, and an haughty spirit before a fall" (Prov. 16: 18, and compare Isa. 1:18). In other cases the truth is driven home by a contrast: "The curse of the Lord is in the house of the wicked: but He blesseth the habitation of the just" (Prov. 3:33, and 15:17). In the Greek emphasis is indicated by the order of words in a sentence: "Now of Jesus Christ the birth was on this wise" (Matt. 1:18); "But commendeth His love toward us" (Rom. 5:8).

The importance of *heeding* the Divine emphasis in intimated in a number of ways. "The verily, verily" with which Christ prefaced some of His weightiest utterances. His use of the interrogative rather than the affirmative in such cases as "What shall it profit a man, if he shall gain the whole world, and lose his own soul?" (Mark 8:36) — so much more forceful than "It would profit a man nothing if," etc. In order to call urgent attention to what He has just said, Christ's "he that hath ears to hear, let him hear" is used again, with a slight variation, in each of His addresses to the seven churches of Revelation 2 and 3. Several notable statements of Paul are prefaced with "This is a faithful saying." When he explains the significance of Melchizedek he gives point to this principle: "*first* being by interpretation King of righteousness, and *after that* also King of Salem, which is, King of peace" (Heb. 7:2, and cf. James 3: 17). For the purpose of impressiveness other declarations are introduced with the word "Behold"; "*Behold,* how good and how pleasant it is for brethren to dwell together in unity!" (Ps. 133:1, and cf. I John 3:1).

19

26. *The origin of words.* An enormous amount of time, research and study has been devoted thereto, and men of great erudition have embodied the results of their labor in volumes which are massive and expensive. Yet in the judgment of the writer they are far from possessing that value which has often been attributed to them, nor does he consider they are nearly as indispensable to the preacher as many have affirmed. Undoubtedly they contain considerable information of interest to etymologists, but as a means for interpreting the Scriptures *lexicons* are greatly overrated. A knowledge of the derivation of the words used in the original Scriptures cannot be essential, for it is unobtainable to the vast majority of God's people. Moreover, the attempts to arrive at such derivations are often not at all uniform, for the best Hebraists are far from being agreed as to the particular roots from which various words in the Old Testament are taken. To us it seems very unsatisfactory, yea, profane, to turn to heathen poets and philosophers to discover how certain Greek words were used before they were given a place in the New Testament. But what is still more to the point, such a method breaks down before the Holy Spirit's actual employment of various terms.

In view of what was said under the eighteenth canon of exegesis, we do not propose to write much on this one. Instead, we will confine ourselves to a single example, which illustrates the closing sentence of the preceding paragraph, and which will at the same time give the lie to an error which is very widespread today. Many of those who deny that the wicked will be punished everlastingly appeal to the fact that the Greek adjective *aionios* simply signifies "age lasting," and that *eis ton aiona* (Jude 13) and *eis aionas aionon* (Rev. 14:11) mean "to the age" and "to the ages of ages" and "for ever" and "for ever and ever." The simple reply is, Granted; yet that is nothing to the point at issue. True, those Greek expressions are but *time terms,* for the sufficient reason that the minds of the ancients were incapable of rising to the concept of *eternity.* Therefore the language employed by those who were destitute of a written revelation from God makes nothing either pro or con concerning the endlessness of the bliss of the redeemed or of the misery of the lost. In order to ascertain *that* we must observe how the terms are used in Holy Writ.

The connections in which the Holy Spirit has employed the word *aionios* leave no room whatever for any uncertainty of its meaning in the mind of an impartial investigator. That word occurs not only in such expressions as "eternal destruction," "everlasting fire," "everlasting punishment," but also in "life eternal" (Matt. 25:46), "eternal salvation" (Heb. 5:9), "eternal glory" (I Peter 5:10); and most assuredly *they are timeless.* Still more decisively, it is linked with the subsistence of

Deity: "the everlasting God" (Rom. 16:26). Again, the force and scope of the word are clearly seen in the fact that it is antithetical to what is of limited duration: "the things which are seen are *temporal*; but the things which are not seen are *eternal*" (II Cor. 4:18). Now it is obvious that if the temporal things lasted forever there could be no contrast between them and the things which are eternal. Equally certain is it that if eternal things be only "age long" they differ not essentially from temporal ones. The contrast between the temporal and the eternal is as real and as great as between the things "seen and unseen." Again, in Philemon 15 *aionios* (rendered "for ever") is set over against "for a season," showing that the one is the very opposite of the other — "receive him for ever" manifestly signifies *never* banish or turn him away.

Before leaving this subject it should be pointed out that the absolute hopelessness of the condition of the lost rests not only on the fact that their punishment is said to be eternal, but on other collateral considerations which are equally final. There is not a single instance recorded in Scripture of a sinner being saved after death, nor any passage holding out any promise of such. On the other hand, there are many to the contrary. "He, that being often reproved hardeneth his neck, shall suddenly be destroyed, and that *without remedy*" (Prov. 29:1), which would not be the case if, after "ages" in purifying fire, he was ultimately admitted into heaven. To His enemies Christ said, "ye . . . shall die in your sins: whither I go, ye cannot come" (John 8:21) — death would seal their doom. That is equally certain from those fearful words of His, "the resurrection of damnation" (John 5:29), which excludes every ray of hope for their recovery in the next life. For the apostate "there remaineth no more sacrifice for sins" (Heb. 10:26). "For he shall have judgment *without mercy*, that hath showed no mercy" (James 2:13). "Whose *end* is destruction" (Phil. 3:19). Therefore is it written at the close of Scripture, "He that is unjust, let him be unjust still: and he which is filthy, let him be filthy still" (Rev. 22:11) — as the tree falls, so will it forever lie.

27. *The law of comparison and contrast.* While this rule is much less important to the expositor than many of the others, it is of deep interest; and though little is known, yet this principle is accorded a prominent place in the Word. And in view of what has been termed "the pair of opposites" which confront us in every sphere, it should occasion us no surprise to find this canon receiving such frequent illustration and exemplification in the Scriptures, and that in several ways. God and the Devil, time and eternity, day and night, male and female, good and evil, heaven and hell, are set one over against the other. "In the beginning God created the heaven *and* the earth, and the earth has its two hemispheres, the northern and the southern. So also there are the Old and New Testaments, the Jew and the Gentile, and after the days of Solomon the former were split into two kingdoms; while throughout all Christendom we find the genuine possessor and the graceless professor. Whatever be the explanation, we are faced everywhere with this mys-

terious duality: the visible and the invisible, spirit and matter, land and sea, centrifugal and centripetal forces at work, life and death.

As pointed out on a previous occasion, Truth itself is ever *twofold,* and hence the Word of God is itself likened to a two-edged sword. Not only is it, first, a revelation from God, and, second, addressed to human responsibility; but a great many passages in it have a twofold force and meaning, a literal and a spiritual; many of its prophecies possess a double fulfilment, a major and a minor; while promise and precept, or privilege and corresponding obligation, are ever combined. Cases of *pairs* are numerous. The two great lights (Gen. 1:16); two of every sort entering the ark (6:19). The two tables on which the Law was written. The two birds (Lev. 14:4-7); the two goats (16:7); the two-tenth deals of fine flour and the two loaves (23:13, 17). The repeated miracle of water from the smitten rock (Exod. 17, Num. 20), as Christ also duplicated the feeding of a great multitude with a few loaves and fishes. The two signs to Gideon (Judg. 6). The two olive trees (Zech. 4). The two masters (Matt. 6:24); the two foundations (7:24-27). The two debtors (Luke 7:41); the two sons (15:11); the two men who went into the temple to pray (18:10). The two false witnesses against Christ (Matt. 26:60); and the two thieves crucified with Him. The two angels (Acts 1:10). The two "immutable things of Hebrews (6:18). The two beasts (Rev. 13).

As Christ sent forth His apostles in pairs, so all through the Bible two individuals are more or less closely associated: in a few instances the one complementing the other, but in the majority there being a marked contrast between them. Thus we have Cain and Abel, Enoch and Noah, Abraham and Lot, Sarah and Hagar, Isaac and Ishmael, Jacob and Esau, Moses and Aaron, Caleb and Joshua, Naomi and Ruth, Samuel and Saul, David and Jonathan, Elijah and Elisha, Nehemiah and Ezra, Martha and Mary, the Pharisees and the Sadducees, Annas and Caiaphas, Pilate and Herod, Paul and Barnabas. Sometimes a series of marked antitheses meet together in the life of a single individual. Notably was this the case with Moses. "He was the child of a slave, and the son of a princess. He was born in a hut, and lived in a palace. He was educated in the court, and dwelt in the desert. He was the mightiest of warriors, and the meekest of men. He had the wisdom of Egypt, and the faith of a child. He was backward in speech, and talked with God. He had the rod of the shepherd, and the power of the infinite. He was the giver of the law, and the forerunner of grace. He died alone on mount Nebo, and appeared with Christ in Judaea. No man assisted at his funeral, yet God buried him" (I. M. Haldeman).

A. T. Pierson pointed out that another series of striking paradoxes is found in that remarkable prophecy of the Messiah in Isaiah 53. Though the Son of God, yet His report was not believed. He appeared to God as "a tender plant," but to men as "a root out of a dry ground." Jehovah's Servant, in whom His soul delighted, but in the esteem of the Jews possessed of no form or comeliness. Appointed by the Father and anointed by the Spirit, yet despised and rejected of men. Sorely wounded and chastised by sinners, yet believing sinners healed by His stripes. No iniquity found in Him, but the iniquities of many were upon Him. Himself the Judge of all, yet brought before the judgment bar of human creatures. Without generation, yet possessing a numerous seed. Cut off out of the land of the living, yet alive for evermore. He made His grave with the wicked, nevertheless He was with the rich in His death. Though counted unrighteous, He makes many righteous. He was spoiled by the strong, yet He spoiled the strong, delivering a multitude of captives out of his hand. He was numbered with and mocked by transgressors, but made intercession for them.

It is indeed remarkable to find the twofoldness of things confronting us so frequently in connection with the plan of redemption. Based upon the work of the great federal heads, the first Adam and the last Adam, with the fundamental covenants connected with them: the covenant of works and the covenant of grace. The last Adam with His two distinct natures, constituting Him the God-man Mediator. Two different genealogies are given of Him, in Matthew 1, and Luke 3. There are His two separate advents: the first in deep humiliation, the second in great glory. The salvation He has provided for His people is twofold: objective and subjective or legal and vital, the one which He did *for* them, and the other which He works *in* them — a righteousness imputed to them, and a righteousness imparted. The Christian life is a strange duality: the principles of sin and grace ever opposing one another. The two ordinances Christ gave to His churches: baptism, and the Lord's supper.

There are many points of contrast between the first two books of the Bible. In the former we have the history of a family; in the latter the history of a nation. In the one the descendants of Abraham are but few in number; in the other they have increased to hundreds of thousands. In Genesis the Hebrews are welcomed and honored in Egypt, whereas in Exodus they are hated and shunned. In the former we read of a Pharaoh who says to Joseph, "God hath showed thee all this" (41:39), but in the latter another Pharaoh says unto Moses, "I know not the Lord" (5:2). In Genesis we hear of a "lamb" promised (22:8), in Exodus of the "lamb" slain and its blood sprinkled. In the former we have recorded the entrance of Israel into Egypt; in the latter the exodus of them is described. In the one we behold the patriarchs sojourning in the land which flowed with milk and honey; in the other their descendants are wanderers in the wilderness. Genesis closes with Joseph in a coffin, while Exodus ends with the glory of the Lord filling the tabernacle.

It is both interesting and instructive to compare the supernatural passages of Israel through the Red Sea and the Jordan. There are at least twelve details of resemblance between them, which we will leave the reader to work out for himself. Here, we will consider their points of dissimilarity. First, the one terminated Israel's exodus from the house of bondage, the other initiated their entrance into the land of promise. Second, the former miracle was wrought in order that they might escape from the Egyptians, the latter to enable them to approach and conquer the Canaanites. Third, in connection with the one the Lord caused the sea to go back by a strong east wind (Exod. 14:21), but with reference to the other no means whatever were employed — to demonstrate that He is not tied to such, but employs or dispenses with them as He pleases. Fourth, the earlier miracle was performed at nighttime (14:21), the latter in broad daylight. Fifth, at the Red Sea multitudes were slain, for the Lord made the waters to return upon the Egyptians so that they "covered the chariots, and the horsemen, and all the host of Pharaoh that came into the sea after them; there remained not so much as one of them" (14:28), whereas at the Jordan not a single soul perished.

Sixth, the one was wrought for a people who just previously had been full of unbelief and murmuring (Exod. 14:11), the other for a people who were believing and obedient (Josh. 2:24; 3:1). Seventh, with the sole exception of Caleb and Joshua, all the adults who benefited from the former miracle died in the wilderness; whereas the great majority of those who were favored to share in the latter "possessed their possessions." Eighth, the waters of the Red Sea were "divided" (Exod. 14:21), those of the Jordan were made to "stand upon an heap" (Josh. 3:13). Ninth, in the former the believer's judicial death unto sin was typed out; in the latter his legal oneness with Christ in His resurrection, followed by a practical entrance into his inheritance. Tenth, consequently, there was no "sanctify yourselves" before the former, but such a call was an imperative requirement for the latter (Josh. 3:5). Eleventh, the response made by Israel's enemies to the Lord's interposition for His people at the Red Sea was, "I will pursue, I will overtake, I will divide the spoil; my lust shall be satisfied upon them" (Exod. 15:9); but in the latter, "It came to pass, when all the kings of the Amorites . . . heard that the Lord had dried up the waters of the Jordan . . . their heart melted, neither was there spirit in them any more" (Josh. 5:1). Twelfth, after the former, "Israel saw the Egyptians dead upon the sea shore" (Exod. 14:30); after the latter, a cairn of twelve stones memorialized the event (Josh. 4:20-22).

Many examples of this principle are to be found by observing closely the details of different incidents which the Holy Spirit has placed *side by side* in the Word. For instance, how sudden and strange is the transition which confronts us as we pass from I Kings 18-19. It is as though the sun were shining brilliantly out of the clear sky, and the next moment, without any warning, black clouds draped the heavens. The contrasts presented in those chapters are sharp and startling. In the former we behold the prophet of Gilead at his best; in the latter we see him at his worst. At the close of the one "the hand of the Lord was on Elijah" as he ran before Ahab's chariot; at the beginning of the other the fear of man was upon him, and he "went for his life." There he was concerned only for the glory of Jehovah, here he is occupied only with self. There he was strong in faith, and the helper of his people; here he gives way to unbelief, and is the deserter of his nation. In the one he boldly confronts the four hundred prophets of Baal undaunted, here he flees panic-stricken from the threats of a single woman. From the mountain top he betakes himself to the wilderness, and from supplicating the Lord that He would vindicate His great name to begging Him to take away his life. Who would have imagined such a tragic sequel? How forcibly does the contrast exhibit and exemplify the frailty and fickleness of the human heart even in a saint!

The work of Elijah and Elisha formed two parts of one whole, the one supplementing the other, and though there are manifest parallels between them there are also marked contrasts. Both of them were prophets, both dwelt in Samaria, both were confronted with much the same situation. The falling of Elijah's mantle upon Elisha intimated that the latter was the successor of the former, and that he was called upon to continue his mission. The first miracle performed by Elisha was identical with the last one wrought by his master: the smiting of the waters of the Jordan with the mantle, so that they parted asunder for him (II Kings 2:8, 14). At the beginning of his ministry Elijah had said to king Ahab, "As the Lord God of Israel liveth, before whom I stand" (I Kings 17:1), and when Elisha came into the presence of Ahab's son he also declared, "As the Lord of hosts liveth, before whom I stand" (II Kings 3:14). As Elijah was entertained by the woman of Zarephath, and rewarded her by restoring her son to life (I Kings 17:23), so Elisha was entertained by a woman at Shunem and rewarded her by restoring her son to life (II Kings 4).

Striking as are the points of agreement between the two prophets, the contrasts in their careers and work are just as vivid. The one appeared suddenly and dramatically on the stage of public action, without a word being told us concerning his origin or how he had been previously engaged; but of the other, the name of his father is recorded, and an account is given of his occupation at the time he received his call into God's service. The first miracle of Elijah was the shutting up of the heavens, so that for the space of three and a half years there was neither dew nor rain according to his word; whereas the first public act of Elisha was to heal the springs of water (II Kings 2:21, 22) and to provide abundance of water for the people (3:20). The principal difference between them is seen in the character of the miracles wrought by and connected with them: the majority of those performed by the former were associated with death and destruction, but the great majority of those attributed to Elisha were works of healing and restoration: the one was more the prophet of judgment, the other of grace. The former was marked by loneliness, dwelling apart from the apostate masses; the latter seems to have spent most of his time in the company of the prophets, presiding over their schools. The one was taken to heaven in a chariot of fire, the other fell sick in old age and died a natural death (22:9).

20

In the last chapter we pointed out that different aspects of Truth are frequently emphasized in the Scriptures by placing two incidents in juxtaposition in order to give point to various differences between them. We gave several illustrations from the Old Testament of *the law of comparison and contrast*: let us now show that the same principle holds good in the New Testament. Consider, first, the striking antitheses between what is recorded in Luke 18:35-42, and 19:1-9. That which is narrated in the former occurred as Christ approached Jericho (the city of the curse — Joshua 6:26), whereas the latter took place after He had passed through it. The subject of the first was a blind beggar, that of the second was "chief of the publicans." Bartimaeus occupied a lowly place, for he "sat by the way side"; Zacchaeus assumed an elevated position, for he "climbed up into a sycomore tree." The one was intent on seeking alms from the passers-by; the other was determined to "see Him" — Christ. Bartimaeus took the initiative and cried "Son of David, have mercy on me"; Christ took the initiative with Zacchaeus, bidding him "come down." The former supplicated for his sight; of the latter Christ made a peremptory request: "today I must abide at thy house." The multitude rebuked Bartimaeus for crying to Christ; all "murmured" at Christ for going to be the guest of Zacchaeus.

There is a striking series of contrasts between what is found in the opening verses of John 3 and John 4. What is recorded in the former occurred in Jerusalem: in the latter the scene is laid in Samaria. In the one we have "a man of the Pharisees, named Nicodemus"; in the other, an unnamed woman. He was a person of distinction, a "master of Israel"; she was of the lower classes, for she came to the well "to draw water." He was a favored Jew, she a despised Samaritan — a semi-heathen. Nicodemus was a man of high reputation, a member of the Sanhedrin; the one with whom Christ dealt in John 4 was a woman of dissolute habits. Nicodemus came to Jesus; Christ waited for the woman at the well, and she had no thought of meeting her Saviour. The former incident took place "by night"; the latter at midday. To the self-righteous Pharisee Christ said, "Ye must be born again"; to the sinner of the Gentiles He told of "the gift of God." Nothing is said of how the former interview ended — apparently Nicodemus was, at that time, unconvinced; the latter went forth and bore testimony unto Christ.

By comparing together what is recorded in the earliest parts of John 12 and 13 some interesting and instructive contrasts are revealed. In the former we read that "they made Him a supper"; in the latter, there is a supper which He appointed. There He is seated at the table; here He arose from it. There He is honored; here He performs the office of a menial. In the one we behold Mary at the feet of the Saviour; in the

121

other we see the Son of God stooping to attend to the feet of His disciples. The feet speak of *the walk*. Christ's feet were anointed with costly ointment; those of the apostles were washed with water. As Christ passed through this world He contracted no pollution: he left it as He entered — "holy, harmless, undefiled" (Heb. 7:26). That His feet were anointed with the fragrant spikenard tells us of the sweet savor which ever ascended from Him to the Father, perfectly glorifying Him in every step of His path. In sharp contrast with His, the walk of the disciples was defiled, and the grime of the way needed to be removed if they were to have "part" or communion with Him (13:8). His feet were anointed *before* theirs were washed, for in all things He must have the "preeminence" (Col. 1:18). In connection with the former Judas complained; in the latter, Peter demurred. Interpretatively the one had Christ's burial in view (12:7); the other adumbrated an important part of His present ministry on high (13:1).

Many illustrations of this principle are found in connection with words and expressions that are used *only twice* in the Scriptures, and startling are the contrasts between them. *Apopnigo* occurs only in Luke 8:7, 33: the one having reference to the seed being choked by thorns; the other where the demon possessed swine were choked in the sea. In Luke 2: 1-5, *apographe* is employed in connection with the Firstborn Himself being enrolled on earth, whereas in Hebrews 12:23, it refers to the Church of the Firstborn enrolled in heaven. *Apokueo* is used in James 1:15, 23: of lust bringing forth sin, and of the Father begetting us with the Word of Truth. *Apolausis* is applied to the things which God has given us to enjoy lawfully (I Tim. 6:17), and to the refusal of Moses to enjoy the unlawful pleasures of sin (Heb. 11:25). *Anthrakia* is found only in John 18:18, where Peter joined Christ's enemies before "a fire of coals," and in 21:9, where the disciples fed before one in the presence of Christ. *Choramakros* is the "far country" into which the prodigal took his journey (Luke 15:13), and a very different one to which Christ went at His ascension (Luke 19:12). *Panoplia* is used of the enemy's "armor" (Luke 11:22), and of the armor Christ has provided for the saints (Eph. 6:11, 13).

There are two references to "the king's dale": in the one Melchizedek brought forth that which symbolized Christ (Gen. 14:17, 18); in the other, Absalom erected a monument to himself (II Samuel 18:18). What a marked (and probably designed) contrast there is between the expressions "there *fell* of the people that day about three thousand men" (Exod. 32:28), and "the same day there were *added* unto them about three thousand souls" (Acts 2:41) — the only occasions where "about three thousand" is used in Scripture. Similar too is this example: "there were with him [David] about four hundred men" (I Sam. 22:2), and there "rose up Theudas, boasting himself to be somebody; to whom a number of men, about four hundred, joined themselves" (Acts 5:36). In I Samuel 28:24), we read of the "fat calf" of the witch of Endor; in Luke 15:23, we are told of "the fatted calf" which was killed for the prodigal son! *Katischuo* occurs only in "the gates of hell shall not prevail against it" — the Church (Matt. 16:18), and "the voice of them and of the chief priests prevailed" (Luke 23:23) with Pilate against Christ, to consent to His crucifixion.

How much we miss through failing to heed carefully that word, "comparing spiritual things with spiritual" (I Cor. 2:13). If we spent more time in prayerfully meditating on the Scriptures, we should oftener have occasion to say with David, "I rejoice at Thy word, as one that findeth great spoil" (Ps. 119:162). It is not to the hurried nor to the cursory reader that its treasures are revealed. What a startling and solemn contrast there is between Christ was "numbered with the transgressors" (Mark 15:28), and Judas was "numbered with" the apostles (Acts 1:17). *Kataluma* is used only in Luke 2:7, where it is rendered "there was no room for them in the *inn*"; and in Luke 22:11, where it is translated "guestchamber" — where the Saviour partook of the passover with His disciples. The woman of Thyatira in Acts 16:14, had her heart opened by the Lord so that she might "take unto her" (which is the meaning of the Greek word rendered "attend") the message of God's servant; but the woman of Thyatira in Revelation 2:20, opened her mouth for the purpose of seducing God's servants! Only twice do we read of the Lord Jesus being *kissed,* and what a contrast: the woman's kiss of devotion (Luke 7:38), Judas' kiss of betrayal (Matt. 26:40)!

In connection with the interpreting of Scripture *the value* of this principle of comparing two things or passages and of observing their variations may be still more definitely seen by placing side by side our Lord's parable of the wedding feast of Matthew 22:1-10, and the parable of the great supper of Luke 14:16-24. The commentators have carelessly assumed that they teach the same thing, but a close examination of them will show that, though they have a number of things in common, they present quite different aspects of Truth: illustrating, respectively, the external, general and powerless call of the Gospel and the internal, particular and effectual call of God. In the former it is "servants" (in the plural number) who are engaged (vv. 3, 4, 6, 8, 10); whereas in the latter it is "that servant" (v. 21), "his servant" (v. 21), "the servant" (vv. 22, 23). It is to be noted that their commissions are not the same: the servants are instructed to "call them that were bidden to the wedding" (v. 3), to "tell them" (v. 4), and to "bid to the marriage" (v. 9), and nothing more; whereas the servant was not only to "say to them that were bidden, Come" (v. 17), but also to "bring in" (v. 21), and to "compel them to come in" (v. 23).

When those distinctions are dully weighed, it should be quite evident that, whereas in Matthew 22 the "servants" are the ministers of God sent forth to preach the Gospel to every creature, "the servant" of Luke 14 is none other than the Holy Spirit, who by His invincible power and effectual operations quickens God's elect into newness of life He alone is able to overcome their natural disrelish for and opposition to Divine things, as He alone is competent to "bring in hither the poor, and the maimed, and the halt, and the blind." Nor could anyone less truly say of his efforts, "Lord, it is done *as* thou hast commanded" (Luke 14:22). As

Christ was the "servant" of the Godhead (Matt. 12:18-20) during the days of His flesh, so the blessed Spirit is the "servant" of Christ during this era (John 16:14; Acts 2:33). This interpretation is further confirmed by the fact that the servants were "entreated spitefully" and even "slain" (Matt. 22:6). Moreover, we read of them, "So those servants went out into the highways, and gathered together all [into the local churches] as many as they found, both *bad* and good" (Matt. 22:10), for they were unable to read hearts; but no such statement is made of the Servant, who "brings" (to heaven) those with whom He deals.

Ere leaving this division of our subject, one other example of its importance and value. By making use of the law of contrast we are able decisively to determine the controversy which Socinians have raised upon that momentous verse, "For He hath made Him to be sin for us, who knew no sin; that we [which were destitute of acceptable obedience] might be made the righteousness of God in Him" (II Cor. 5:21). That is one of the profoundest and most comprehensive statements to be found in the Scriptures concerning the atonement, containing as it does a brief epitome of the whole plan of salvation. Enemies of the Gospel insist that the "made sin" ought to be translated "made a sin-offering," but such is entirely inadmissible, for in that case the antithesis would require us to render "that we might be made a righteous-offering of God in Him" — a manifest absurdity. The contrast which is here drawn fixes the exact meaning of the terms used. Believers are legally constituted righteous in Christ before God, and therefore the contrast *demands* that Christ was legally constituted sin — guilty in the eyes of God's Law. The grand truth affirmed in this verse is the exchange of places with the counter imputations thereof: our sins were reckoned to the account of our Surety, rendering Him judicially guilty; His obedience is reckoned to our account, rendering us judicially righteous before God.

28. *The law of first mention.* Very frequently this is of great help in arriving at the meaning of a word or expression. Since there be but one Speaker throughout the entire Word, and He knew from the beginning all that He was going to say, He has so ordered His utterances as to forecast from the outset whatever was to follow. Thus, by noting its setting and associations, the initial occurrence of anything in the Scriptures usually intimates to us how it subsequently will be employed. In other words, the earliest pronouncement of the Holy Spirit on a subject very frequently indicates, substantially, what is found in the later references thereto. This is of real assistance to the expositor, supplying him with a kind of key to what follows. So far as we are aware, attention was originally directed to this canon of exegesis by Lord Bacon (1600), and for more than forty years this writer has made use of the same, putting it to the test in scores of instances; and while he has found a few cases where the first mention of a term failed to intimate clearly its future scope, he has never met with one that was out of harmony therewith; and the vast majority of them were invaluable in serving to define their significance and scope. This will appear from the illustrations which follow.

The *first prophecy* recorded in Scripture supplies the key to the whole subject of Messianic prediction, furnishing a remarkable outline and forecast of all that was to follow. Said the Lord God to the serpent, "And I will put enmity between thee and the woman, and between thy seed and her seed; it shall bruise thy head, and thou shalt bruise his heel" (Gen. 3:15). First, it is to be noted that those words were not addressed to Adam and Eve, implying that man was not the immediate party in the covenant of recovery; that it depended not upon anything of, by or from *him*. Second, that this Divine pronouncement was made after the fall, and from this point onwards prophecy is always consequent upon human failure, not coming in during the normal state of affairs, but only when ruin has begun and judgment is impending — the next prophecy was through Enoch (Jude 14, 15) just before the flood! In the prophecy of Genesis 3:15, it was revealed that all human hope was to center in a Coming One. It made known that the Coming One should be man, the woman's "seed," and therefore of supernatural birth. It announced that He would be the object of Satan's enmity. It foretold that He should be temporarily humiliated — bruised in His heel. It also proclaimed His ultimate victory, for He should bruise the serpent's head, and therfore must be more than man. It intimated the age-long strife there would be between the two seeds: the children of the Devil and those united unto Christ.

And the Lord said unto Cain, "What hast thou done? the voice of thy brother's blood crieth unto Me from the ground" (Gen. 4:10). That is the first time that all-important word "blood" is mentioned in the Scriptures, and like all the initial occurrences of fundamental terms it well repays the most careful attention and meditation. Profoundly important is this reference, foreshadowing as it does some of the most essential and outstanding features of the atonement of Christ. Abel was a shepherd (Gen. 4:2) and was hated, though without cause, by his brother (I John 3:12). He did not die a natural death, but met with a violent end: as the good Shepherd was crucified and slain by wicked hands (Acts 2:23). In the light of those facts, how deeply significant are the words "the voice of thy brother's blood *crieth unto Me*." That is the all-important but inexpressibly blessed thing in connection with the blood of Christ: it is *vocal Godwards!* It is "the blood of sprinkling, that speaketh better things than that of Abel" (Heb. 12:24), for it satisfied every demand of God and procured inestimable blessing for His people. The next mention of "blood" is in Genesis 9:4, where we learn that *life* is in the blood. The third reference is Exodus 12:13, where it delivers from the avenging angel. Put the three together and we have a complete outline of all the subsequent teaching of Scripture upon the blood. They treat, respectively, of death, life, salvation.

21

THE first time that center of man's moral nature — *the heart* — is mentioned in the Scriptures we have an infallible forecast of all later teaching thereon. "And God saw that the wickedness of man was great in the earth, and that every imagination of the thoughts of his heart was only evil continually" (Gen. 6:5). Remarkably full is the outline here furnished us. Observe first the words "and God saw," intimating that He alone is fully conversant with this inward spring from which proceed the issues of life. Second, that it is upon the same His eyes are fixed: "man looketh on the outward appearance, but the Lord looketh on the heart" (I Sam. 16:7). Third, that what is here said of man's heart is *explanatory of* his wicked conduct: since the fount itself be foul, filthy must be the streams flowing therefrom. Fourth, that man's heart is now radically evil, and that continually, being "deceitful [the Hebrew word is rendered "crooked" in Isa. 40:4, and "polluted" in Hosea 6:8] . . . and desperately [incurably] wicked" (Jer. 17:9); out of which, as Christ declared, proceed all the abominations committed by fallen man (Mark 7:21-23). Fifth, that the "heart" equals the whole of the inner man, for the marginal rendering of "every imagination of the thoughts of his heart" is "the purposes and desires," and thus it is not only the seat of his thought, but that of his affections and will.

"And it repented the Lord that He had made man on the earth, and it grieved Him at His heart. And the Lord said, I will destroy man whom I have created from the face of the earth" (Gen. 6:6, 7). This is the initial reference to *repentance,* and though its language be indeed metaphorical — for by a figure of speech (anthropopathia) the Lord ascribes to Himself human feelings — yet it contains all the essential elements thereof. First it is striking to find that this grace is here attributed not to the creature, but to the Creator, telling us that repentance originates not in one whose mind is enmity against God and whose heart is hard as a stone, but is a Divine gift (Acts 5:31; 11:18; II Tim. 2:25), wrought in him by the Holy Spirit. Second, that repentance has *sin* for its object. for it is the wickedness of men which is here said to make Jehovah repent. Third, *its nature* is clearly defined: as a change of mind (God's repenting that He had made man) and a grief of heart. Fourth, that the genuineness of repentance is evidenced by *reformation,* or an alteration of conduct, a resolve to undo (as far as is humanly possible) that which is sorrowed over — seen in the Lord's decision to destroy man from off the face of the earth.

In Genesis 15:6, we find the earliest mention of three of the most important words which are used in connection with the sinner's salvation, and most significant and blessed is it to see them here joined together. "And he [Abraham] believed in the Lord; and He counted it to him for righteousness." What a remarkable anticipation was this of the fuller unfolding of the Gospel which is to be found in the Prophets and the New Testament! It records the response made by "the father of all them that believe" (Rom. 4:11) to the amazing promise which Jehovah made to him: that, despite his being so old (almost one hundred years), he should not only beget a son, but ultimately have an innumerable seed, and that from the same should spring the Messiah. As Romans 4:19, 20, states, "he considered not his body now dead . . . he staggered not at the promise of God through unbelief; but was strong in faith, giving glory to God." First, here we have the simplest definition of faith to be found in the Bible: "he believed in the Lord." More literally, "he *amened* Jehovah": that is to say, his heart gave the answering assurance "it shall be so." In other words, by implicitly receiving the Divine testimony, he "set to his seal that God is true" (John 3:33). He realized that it was the word of Him "that cannot lie."

Second, we here learn what was God's gracious response to that childlike confidence which so honored Him: "He counted it to him for righteousness." The word "counted" means accounted or placed to his credit; the same Hebrew word being translated "imputeth'" Ps. 32:2: "Blessed is the man unto whom the Lord imputeth not iniquity" — charges it not against him. It is *not the act* of Abraham's faith which is here referred to, but the glorious Object to which it looked, namely, his promised Seed and Son — his Saviour. Third, we are here taught how a believing sinner is legally constituted just before God. By nature he has no righteousness of his own, for so long as he be without Christ, his best performances are but as filthy rags in the sight of Divine holiness. Not only was Abraham destitute of righteousness, but he obtained it not by any efforts of his own: his faith was the sole means or instrument which linked him to a righteousness outside of himself. After citing his case, the apostle went on to say, "Even as David also describeth the blessedness of the man, unto whom God imputeth righteousness *without works*" (Rom. 4:6), "for with the heart man believeth *unto* righteousness" (Rom. 10:10).

Since the above treats of such a vital aspect of the Truth, we will link with it and consider briefly Deuteronomy 25:1. "If there be a controversy between men, and they come unto judgment, that the judges may judge them; then they shall *justify* the righteous, and condemn the wicked." That is the first occurrence of this important word, and its setting more than hints at its meaning. First, justification is entirely a judicial matter, being the sentence of pronouncement of the Judge of all the earth. Second, it is the opposite of condemnation, and when one is condemned in the law courts he is not made wicked, but adjudged guilty. Third, he is regarded as "righteous," that is the Law has nothing against him — because in the believer's case all its requirements have been fully met by his Surety. We may also consider in this connection, "Stand still, and see the salvation of the Lord, which He will show to you today: for the Egyptians whom ye have seen today, ye shall see them again no more forever" (Exod. 14:13). How deeply significant is that first mention of "salvation," containing as it does all the prime elements of our spiritual deliverance. It was the Lord's salvation, in which they had no part or hand, yea, they had to cease from all activity in order to see the same. It consisted of a miraculous deliverance from death. It was a present thing, which they experienced that day. It was complete and eternal, for they would see their enemies again "no more for ever."

Most suggestive is the initial reference to the *lamb*. "And he said, Behold the fire and the wood: but where is the lamb for a burnt offering?" (Gen. 22:7, 8). How blessed and significant to observe, in the first place, that this conversation was between a loving father and an only begotten son (Heb. 11:17). Second, how remarkable to learn that the lamb would not be demanded from man, but supplied by God. Third, still more noteworthy are the words "God will *provide Himself* a lamb," because it was for the meeting of *His* requirements, the satisfying of His claims. Fourth, the lamb was not here designed for food (for that was not the prime thought), but "for a burnt offering." Fifth, it was a substitute for the child of promise, for, as verse 13 exhibits, "the ram" (a male lamb in the prime of its strength) was not only provided by God, but was also offered by Abraham "in the stead of his son"! How significant it is to discover that the word *worship* is mentioned for the first time in connection with this scene: "I and the lad will go yonder and worship, and will come again to you" (v. 5). Worship calls for separation from unbelievers, as Abraham left his two young men behind him; it is possible only on resurrection ground ("the third day" v. 4); and it consists of offering unto God our best — our Isaac.

How indicative are the opening words of our Bible: "In the beginning God." Here man is taught the first grand truth which he needs to know: that God is first and foremost, the Author of all things: the source and spring of all good. The first appearance of Satan in Scripture reveals to us his subtle character, the methods he employs, that God's Word is the chief object of his assaults, and stamps him as the arch-liar. How the first recorded words of the Redeemer, "Wist ye not that I must be about My Father's business?" (Luke 2:49), summed up His mission and all His subsequent teaching, as well as intimated that such would be neither appreciated nor understood by men. Many other illustrations of this law of first mention might be given, but the above are amply sufficient to exemplify its reality and value. They reveal how important it is to trace things back to their source, and show that God has hung the key on the door for us to make use of. And they demonstrate the Divine authorship of the Bible, displaying as they do that the later books invariably employ terms and phrases with uniform significance and in perfect harmony with their initial mention. What proofs that He who knew the end from the beginning inspired holy men of old in the very words they selected and the use which they made of them.

29. *The law of progress.* Since the Scriptures be the "word of life" (Phil. 2:16), they are "quick [living], and powerful" (Heb. 4:12). So far from being "a dead book" as the papists blasphemously assert, and "a dead letter" as some Protestants have ignorantly averred, the Bible

is instinct with the very life of its Author. This fact is plainly exemplified in the principle of *growth* which marks all its parts and itself as a whole. This can be tested and verified by any competent person who will take the trouble to read the Scriptures systematically, or trace out a subject from start to finish. As this be done, he will perceive that Truth is unfolded orderly and gradually, progressively and climactically: that there is presented to us first the blade, then the ear, and after that the full corn in the ear. While the first mention of a thing intimates its scope and more or less anticipates what is to follow, the subsequent references amplify the same, each one making its own contribution to the whole, and thereby we obtain both a clearer and a fuller understanding of the same. The path of Truth is like that of the just: it "shineth more and more."

As we pointed out nearly forty years ago, the above-named principle is strikingly and blessedly illustrated in connection with the Lamb. In Genesis 22:8, the lamb is *prophesied*: "God *will* provide Himself a lamb." In Exodus 12 the lamb is clearly *typified*, as "without blemish," whose blood provided shelter from the destroying angel, and whose flesh was to be the food of God's people. In Isaiah 53:7, the lamb is definitely *personified*: "*He* is brought as a lamb to the slaughter." In John 1:29, we find the lamb *identified*, as pointing to Him, Christ's forerunner announced "Behold the Lamb of God, which taketh away the sin of the world." In I Peter 1:19, mention is made of Him as the lamb that was *crucified*: "But with the precious blood of Christ, as of a lamb without blemish and without spot." In Revelation 5:6, we see the Lamb *glorified*, for the seer of Patmos was privileged to behold in heaven, standing, "a Lamb as it had been slain." While in Revelation 22:1, we see the Lamb *satisfied*: "And He showed me a pure river of water of life, clear as crystal, proceeding out of the throne of God and of the Lamb." With these we may link the progressive scope seen in the validity of Christ's sacrifice. In Genesis 4:4, for the individual; in Exodus 12:3, for the "house" or family; in Leviticus 16:21, for the nation; in Ephesians 5:25, for the Church or the whole election of grace.

Another example of this law of progress may be seen by tracing out the Messianic prophecies and observing how there is "line upon line" until the picture is complete. The subject is too vast to deal with comprehensively here, but let us look at a single aspect of it, namely those which respect His *birth*. In Genesis 3:15, it was intimated that the destroyer of Satan would be a member of the human race — the woman's seed. Genesis 9:27, revealed which of the three main divisions of the human race He would descend from: "He [God] shall dwell in the tents of Shem." In Genesis 22:18, it was made known that He should be an Israelite — Abraham's seed. II Samuel 7:12, 13, announced that He should be of the tribe of Judah — issuing from David. Isaiah 11:10, defined His ancestry yet more definitely: He would spring from the family of Jesse. Isaiah 49:1, predicted that He would be *named*, and by God Himself, *before* His birth, as indeed He was. While Micah 5:2, specified the very place where he would be born — Bethlehem. Such examples as these not only demonstrate clearly the Divine inspiration of the Bible, but evidence that the canon of Scripture, as we now have it, has been superintended by God Himself, for its order is not so much chronological as logical.

There is a steady advance observable in the respective purposes and scope of *the four Gospels*. Obviously, Matthew's must come first, for its chief design is to present Christ as the Embodiment of the Old Testament promises and the Fulfiller of the prophecies there made concerning the Messiah. For much the same reason Mark's comes second, for whereas in the former Christ is seen *testing* the old covenant people, here He is viewed as *ministering to* them. But Luke's Gospel has a much wider scope, being far more Gentile in its character. In it Christ is contemplated in connection with the human race: the Son of man related to yet contrasted with the sons of men. John's Gospel conducts us to much higher ground, for whereas in the first three He is depicted in human relationships (as the Son of Abraham, the Servant of God, and the perfect Man), here His Divine glory shines forth and we behold Him as the Son of God in relation to the family of God. This same principle is also exemplified in what is recorded in *their closing chapters*. Matthew takes us no farther than the resurrection of Christ; in Mark 16:19, mention is made of His ascension; in Luke 24:49, promise is given of the coming of the Spirit on the day of Pentecost; while John's Gospel ends with a reference to His second coming!

The predictive announcements which the Saviour made to His disciples of His forthcoming sufferings observe this principle, being *cumulative* in their respective revelations. "From that time forth began Jesus to show unto His disciples, how that He must go unto Jerusalem, and suffer many things of the elders and chief priests and scribes, and be killed" (Matt. 16:21). That supplied a general outline — in keeping with the law of first mention. "And while they abode in Galilee, Jesus said unto them, The Son of man shall be betrayed into the hands of men: and they shall kill Him" (17:22, 23). Here the additional fact of His being betrayed was mentioned. "And the Son of man shall be betrayed unto the chief priests and unto the scribes, and they shall condemn Him to death, and shall deliver Him to the Gentiles to mock, and to scourge, and to crucify Him" (20:18, 19): here He enlarged upon the horrible indignities which He would suffer. "Then saith Jesus unto them, All ye shall be offended because of Me this night" (26:31). There the perfidy of His own disciples was foretold. How like the Saviour it was to break the sad news to them gradually! What consideration for their feelings!

It is to be noted that in those announcements, as in all the other references which He made to His passion, the Lord spoke only of the *human* side thereof, being entirely silent upon the Godward aspect. In perfect accord with this law of progress, we have to proceed beyond the Gospels (which give a historical account of the external facts) to the Epistles, where the Spirit (sent to guide the apostles into "all truth") makes known the spiritual design and internal meaning of the Cross. There we are informed that the death of Christ was both a propitiatory and an expiatory one: a satisfaction unto Divine justice, a sacrifice which put away the sins of God's people. So too in the Epistles themselves we find that, while in the earlier ones the *individual* effects and blessings of redemption are more in view, in the later ones the individual is no longer prominent, rather is he seen as a part of a greater whole — a member of the body of Christ. True, in the earlier ones the individual is not ignored. But the *proportion* of the two aspects has changed: what is primary in the former becomes secondary in the latter. That is the natural order in the development of Truth.

22

30. *The law of full mention.* We have treated the principle of first mention, and showed that the initial reference to a subject or the earliest occurrence of a term indicated from its context and the manner in which it was used would be its force in all later references. This we followed with the law of progressive mention, wherein it was seen that the Holy Spirit has observed an orderly development in the unfolding of each aspect of the Truth; that as it is naturally, so in connection with Divine revelation: there is first the blade, then the ear, after that the full corn in the ear. That may be further illustrated by a simple and well-known example, namely the three allusions made to Nicodemus in John's Gospel. In John 3 we behold the midnight condition of his soul; in 7:50, 51, we see, as it were, the dawning of twilight; but in 19:39, 40, the daylight had fully broken. Now those principles are augmented by a third, for, as A. T. Pierson pointed out in his most helpful book *The Bible and Spiritual Criticism* (now out of print), somewhere in the Bible each of its prominent themes is given a complete and systematic presentation. In other words, a whole chapter is devoted to an exhaustive treatment of what is more briefly mentioned elsewhere. Below, we barely mention examples of this fact — culled from Dr. Pierson, supplemented by our own researches.

Exodus 20 gives us the complete Decalogue, the ten commandments of the moral law being stated clearly and orderly. Psalm 119 sets forth at length the authority, the importance and the manifold excellency of the written Word of God. In Isaiah 53 we have a full-length picture of the vicarious sufferings of the Saviour. John 17 contains a complete outline on the subject of intercession, revealing as it does the substance of those things which our great High Priest asks of the Father for His people. In Romans 3:10-20, we have the most detailed diagnosis of the depraved condition of fallen man to be met with in the Bible. In Romans 5:12-21, the foundation doctrine of federal headship is developed at length. In Romans 7 the conflict between the "two natures" in the believer is described as it is nowhere else. In Romans 9 the awful sovereignty of God, in election or reprobation, is dealt with more largely than elsewhere. In I Corinthians 15 the resurrection of the believer's body is depicted in its full-robed splendor. In II Corinthians 8 and 9 every aspect of Christian giving and the varied motives which should prompt our benevolences are stated. In Hebrews 2:6-18, we find the clearest and most comprehensive setting forth of the reality of our Lord's humanity. In Hebrews 11 we have a wonderfully complete outline of the life of faith. Hebrews 12 furnishes us with an extensive treatment of the subject of Divine chastisement. In James 3 we have summed up what the rest of the Bible teaches concerning the might and

malice of the tongue. The whole of Jude is devoted to the solemn theme
of apostasy.

In these chapters we have endeavored to set before our readers those
rules which we have long made use of in our own study of the Word.
Since they were designed more especially for young preachers, we have
spared no efforts to make them as lucid and complete as possible, placing in their hands those principles of exegesis which have stood us in
best stead. Though not a distinct canon of hermeneutics, a few remarks
require to be offered on the subject of *punctuation*, for since there be
none in the original manuscripts, the manner and mode of dividing the
text is often a matter of interpretation. The early copies were unbroken
into chapters and verses, still less had they any notations of their sentences and clauses. It should also be pointed out that the use of large
capitals in such verses as Exodus 3:14; 27:3; Isaiah 26:4; Jeremiah 23;
Zechariah 14:20; Revelation 17:6; 19:16, originated with the Authorized
Version of 1611, for they are not found in any of the previous transla-
tions. They are without any authority, and were used to indicate what
the translators deemed to be of particular importance.

The use of parentheses is entirely a matter of interpretation, for there
were none in the originals and few in the early Greek copies. The
translators deemed them necessary in a few instances, so as to indicate
the sense of a passage by preserving the continuity of thought, as in
Romans 5:13-17, which is an unusually long one. Some of the simplest
and best known examples are Matthew 6:32; Luke 2:35; John 7:50;
Romans 1:2. It is not to be thought that words enclosed in brackets are
of less importance: sometimes they are an amplification, as in Mark 5:
13; at others they are explanatory, as in Mark 5:42; John 4:2. Instead
of being only of trivial significance, a number of parenthetical clauses
are of deep moment. For instance, "For I know that in myself (that is
in my flesh,) dwelleth no good thing" (Rom. 7:18) — the absence of that
qualifying word had denied that there was any principle of grace or
holiness in him. Similar examples are found in II Corinthians 5:7,
and 6:2. On the other hand, some are of doubtful propriety: not all will
consider that the parentheses found in the following passages are necessary or even expedient: Mark 2:10; John 1:14, and 7:39; I Corinthians
9:21; II Corinthians 10:4; Ephesians 4:9, 10. Below are three passages
in which this writer considers the use of parentheses is a real help in
the understanding of them.

In our judgment a threefold change is required in the punctuation of
I Corinthians 15:22-26. First, the clause "then cometh the end" should
be placed at the close of verse 23 and not at the beginning of verse 24,
for it completes the sentence instead of beginning a new one. Second,
the whole of verse 25 requires to be placed in brackets if the order of
thought is to be preserved. Third, the italicized words in verses 24 and
26 should be deleted, for they are not only unnecessary, but misleading.
Punctuated thus, the passage will read: "For as in Adam all die, even so
in Christ shall all be made alive; but every man [literally "everyone"] in
his own order: Christ the firstfruits, afterward they that are Christ's at

His coming, then the end." As the sin of Adam resulted not only in his own death, but also in the deaths of all who were in him as their federal head, so the obedience unto death of Christ not only procured His own resurrection, but ensures that of all who are united to Him as their federal Head: a resurrection in honor and glory — the resurrection of the wicked "to shame and everlasting contempt" falls not within the scope of this chapter. The clause "then the end" denotes *not* "the termination of all mundane affairs," but signifies the conclusion of the resurrection — the completion of the harvest (John 12:24).

By placing its first clause at the close of verse 23, what follows in verse 24 begins a fresh sentence, though not a new subject. "When He shall have delivered up the kingdom to God [not His mediatorial one, but only that aspect thereof which concerns the suppression of all re-volters against heaven], even the Father; when He shall have put down all rule and all authority and power (for He must reign till He hath put down all enemies under His feet), the last enemy shall be destroyed — death." Christ rose again *to reign*: all power in heaven and in earth has been given to Him for the express purpose of subjugating and annulling all the enemies of Himself and of His Father, and this issues in the aboli-tion of death in the glorious resurrection of all His people. The grand object throughout this chapter is to show the guarantee which Christ's resurrection gives for that of His redeemed — *denied* by some (v. 12). That this subject is continued *after* the passage we are here critically ex-amining is clear from verses 29-32, where further arguments are advanced — from the case of those who are baptized and Paul's own experiences. Verses 24-26 are brought in to assure the hearts of believers: many powerful enemies seek to bring about their destruction, but their efforts are utterly vain, for Christ shall triumph over them all — death itself be-ing abolished at their resurrection.

Most of the commentators have experienced difficulty when attempting to trace the course of the apostle's argument in Hebrews 4:1-11. Its structure is indeed much involved, but not a little light is cast on it by placing verses 4-10 in parentheses. The exhortation begun in 3:12, is not completed till 4:12, is reached: all that intervenes consists of an ex-position and application of the passage quoted from Psalm 95 in 3:7-11. The connecting link between the two chapters is found in, "So we see that they could not enter in because of unbelief" (3:19). On those words is based the admonition of 4:1-3, which bids us to take to heart the solemn warning there given. The first clause of verse 3, when literally rendered, reads: "For we enter into the rest, who believe" — the historical tense is thus avoided. It is neither "have entered" nor "shall enter," but an abstract statement of a doctrinal fact — only believers enter into God's rest. The second half of 4:3, quotes again from Psalm 95.

In the parentheses of 4:4-10, the apostle enters upon a discussion of the "rest" which the Psalmist spoke of and which he was exhorting his readers to strive to enter, bidding them to take heed lest they fell short of attaining thereto. First, he pointed out (vv. 4-6) that David had not referred to God's own rest upon creation and the Sabbath rest which ensued therefrom. Second, nor was it the rest of Canaan (vv. 7, 8) into which Joshua led Israel. Third, it was something then *future* (v. 9), namely the rest announced in the Gospel. Fourth, in verse 10 there is a noticeable change of number from the "us" in verse 1 and the "we" of verse 3 to "He that is entered into His rest," where the reference is to Christ Himself — *His* entrance being both the pledge and proof that His people will do so: "whither the forerunner is *for us* entered" (6:20). In 4:11, the apostle returns to his principal exhortation of 3:13, and 4:1-3. There he had said, "Let us therefore fear, lest a promise being left us of entering into His rest, any of you should seem to come short of it"; here he makes known *how* that "fear" is to exert itself: not in dread or doubting, but a reverential respect to the Divine threatenings and promises, with a diligent use of the appointed means of grace.

"Who needeth not daily, as those high priests, to offer up sacrifice (first for his own sins, and then for the people's): for this He did once, when He offered up Himself" (Heb. 7:27). This is another verse which has troubled commentators, but all difficulty is removed by inserting the above parentheses. In this and the next verse, the apostle specifies some of the respects in which our High Priest is superior to the priests of the Aaronic order. His perfections, described in verse 26, exempted Him from all the infirmities and blemishes which pertain to the Levitical priests, and which disqualified them from making an effectual atonement unto God for sin. In blessed contrast, Christ was infinitely well pleasing to God: not only without personal transgression and defilement, but intrinsically holy in Himself. Thus, not only was there no need for Him to offer any sacrifice for Himself, but His oblation for His people was of infinite value and eternal validity. "This He did once" announces the glorious fact of its absolute sufficiency: that it requires no repetition on His part, nor augmentation from us.

32) *The use of italics* is also largely a matter of interpretation. In ordinary literature they are employed for emphasis, but in our Bibles they are inserted by the translators with the design of making the sense clearer. Sometimes they are helpful, sometimes harmful. In the Old Testament it is, in certain instances, more or less necessary, for the Hebrew has no copulative, but joins the subject to the predicate, which gives an emphasis of abruptness to which the English mind is unaccustomed, as in "From the sole of the foot even unto the head — no soundness in it. . . . Your country — desolate, your cities — burned with fire" (Isa. 1:6, 7). In the great majority of cases this writer *ignores* the added words of men, considering it more reverent so to do, as well as obtaining more directly the force of the original. In some instances the translators quite missed the real thought of the passage, as in the last clause of Exodus 2, where "God had respect unto them" ought to be "had respect unto *it*," i.e., "His covenant with Abraham, with Isaac and with Jacob" of the previous verse. The last word of Daniel 11:32, is too restrictive — doing His will also is included.

But it is in the New Testament that the majority of mistakes occur. There we find a number of passages where needless additions have been made and where the meaning has been misapprehended, falsified, by the words the translators inserted. In Romans 8:27, "the *will* of God" is too contracted — His covenant, His word, His grace and mercy are not to be excluded. The "from another" in I Corinthians 4:7, unduly narrows the scope — from what *you* were as unregenerate is not to be excluded. "Inspirer" is preferable to "author" in I Corinthians 14:33, for God is the Decreer of all things (Rom. 11:36), yet not the Prompter of confusion. It is very doubtful if "the nature of" is permissible in Hebrews 2:16, for is it not the Divine incarnation which is there in view (*that* we have in v. 14), but rather the purpose and consequence of the same. Its opening "For" looks back, remotely, to verses 9 and 10; immediately, to verses 14 and 15. In verse 16 a reason is given why Christ tasted death for "every *son*," and why He destroyed (annulled the power of) the Devil in order to liberate his captives: it was because He laid hold of (espoused) not the cause of (the fallen) angels, but the chosen seed of Abraham — thus a foundation is here laid for what is said in verse 17.

II Corinthians 6:1, is a yet worse instance, for by inserting the words "with Him" a thought entirely foreign to the apostle's scope is introduced, and ground given for horrible boasting. Paul was referring to the joint efforts of God's servants: the one planting and another watering (I Cor. 3:5, 6). To say they were "workers together with God" would be to divide the honors. If any supplement be made, it should be *under* Him. The ministers of the new covenant were fellowworkers, merely "helpers" of the joy (1:24) of God's people. So too the correct punctuation (as the Greek requires) of I Corinthians 3:9, is: "For God's *we* are: fellow workers; God's heritage *ye* are." One other example must suffice. The added "to bring us" in Galatians 3:24, quite misses the scope of the passage, and inculcates false doctrine. The apostle was not there treating with the experiential side of things, but the *dispensational* (as the opening verses of the next chapter demonstrate); not with the unsaved as such, but with God's people under the old covenant. The Law never brought a single sinner to Christ: the Holy Spirit does *that*, and though He employs the Law to convict souls of their need of Christ, the Gospel is the means which He employs to make them close with Christ.

Now one or two brief observations and we conclude. The work of the expositor is to bring out the grammatical and spiritual meaning of each verse he deals with. In order to do that he must approach it without bias or prejudice, and diligently *study* it. He must neither assume that he knows its meaning nor take his doctrinal views from others. Nor is he to form his own opinions from a few detached verses, but carefully compare his ideas with the entire Analogy of Faith. Each verse requires to be critically examined, and every word thoroughly weighed. Thus he is to note the "*is* accepted" of Acts 10:35, and not "shall be," and the "are" (rather than "shall be") in Hebrews 3:6, 14 — to change the tense mentally in those verses would inculcate false doctrine. Minute care is needed if we are to observe the "the Lord and Saviour" of II Peter 2:20 (not "their"), and the "our" and not "your" of I Corinthians 15:3. Finally, it is not the interpreter's province to explain what God has *not explained* (Deut. 29:29), i.e., His "ways" (Rom. 11:33), miracles, etc.

INDEXES

Index of Scripture

Index of Authors